It's another Quality Book from CGP

This book is for anyone studying Food Technology at GCSE.

Let's face it, D&T is pretty hard-going — you've got a whole load of technical stuff to learn on top of doing your project.

Happily this CGP book helps to take the headache out of all that learning. We've explained all the technical stuff — and drawn plenty of pictures to make the whole thing that bit clearer. Plus we've stuck in some handy hints to help make your project a winner.

And in true CGP style it's got some daft bits in to try and make the whole experience at least vaguely entertaining for you.

What CGP is all about

Our sole aim here at CGP is to produce the highest quality books — carefully written, immaculately presented and dangerously close to being funny.

Then we work our socks off to get them out to you — at the cheapest possible prices.

Contributors:
Marian Brown
Charley Darbishire
Dominic Hall
Angela Nugent
Karen Steel
Martin Chester
Chris Dennett
Simon Little
Andy Park
Claire Thompson

With thanks to Rosemary Cartwright, Marian Brown, Taissa Csaky, Tim Major, Katherine Reed and Glenn Rogers for the proofreading

ISBN-10: 1 84146 790 1
ISBN-13: 978 1 84146 790 0
Groovy website: www.cgpbooks.co.uk

Jolly bits of clipart from CorelDRAW®

Printed by Elanders Hindson Ltd., Newcastle upon Tyne.

Text, design, layout and original illustrations
© Coordination Group Publications Ltd 2002
All rights reserved.

Published by Coordination Group Publications Ltd.

Contents

Section One — The Design Process
Design Brief 1
Research 2
Design Specification 3
Generating Proposals 4
Development 5
Evaluation 6
Manufacturer's Specification 7
Planning Production 8
Revision Summary for Section One 9

Section Two — Materials & Components
Carbohydrates — Sugar 10
Carbohydrates — Starch 11
Carbohydrates — Cereals and Flour 12
Carbohydrates — Wheat 13
Proteins — Meat 14
Proteins — Fish and Alternatives 15
Vitamins and Minerals 16
Fruit and Vegetables 17
Fats and Oils 18
Dairy Products 19
Eggs 20
Revision Summary for Section Two 21

Section Three — Food Processes
Combining Ingredients 22
Different Types of Production 23
Food Contamination and Bacteria 24
Preservation 25
HACCP 26
Setting up Simple HACCP 27
Domestic Equipment 28
Industrial Equipment 29
Revision Summary for Section Three 30

Section Four — Marketing and Industry
Different Target Groups 31
Other Factors Affecting People's Choices 32
Standard Food Components 33
Labelling 34
Packaging 35
Revision Summary for Section Four 36

Section Five — Design and Development
Evaluation and Development 37
Data Collection and Analysis 39
Questionnaires 40
Presenting and Analysing Results 41
Product Analysis 42
Sensory Analysis 43
Control Systems and Feedback 44
Quality Control and Assurance 45
Revision Summary for Section Five 46

Section Six — Project Advice
Tips on Getting Started 47
Tips on Development 48
Tips on Evaluation 49
Tips on Presentation 50
Digital Camera 51
Summary Checklist 52

Index 53

Section One — The Design Process

Design Brief

The process of designing and making something is called 'the design process' (gosh). The whole process can take a while — so, like many pineapples, it's usually broken down into smaller chunks.

The Design Process is Similar in Industry and School

It's no accident that the things you'll have to do for your Design and Technology project are pretty similar to what happens in industry.

- The best products are those that address a real need.
- That's why companies spend so much time and money on customer research. The more people there are who would actually use a product, the more chance it stands of being a roaring success.
- The best ideas for Design and Technology projects are also those that meet a genuine need.

The rest of this section describes a typical design process.
It shows the sort of thing that happens in industry every day.
It also shows the stages you need to go through while you're putting a Design and Technology project together.

First get your Idea for a New Product

First things first... whether you're working in the research and development department of a multinational company, or you're putting together your project, you need to explain why a new product is needed.

It could be for one of the following reasons:

1) There are problems with an existing product.
2) The performance of an existing design could be improved.
3) There's a gap in the market that you want to fill.

The Design Brief explains Why your Product is Needed

The design brief explains why there might be a need for a new product.
It should include the following:

1) an outline of the problem and who it affects
2) the need arising from the problem
3) what you intend to do about it (e.g. design and make...)
4) how your product will be used
5) the environment it will be used in

Design Brief for Double Lard Chocolate Cake

There is no cake available that uses the great flavour of lard.

So we will manufacture a cake that combines lard with the already popular flavour of chocolate.

Basically, the design brief should concentrate on the problem you're trying to solve.

Remember — your project doesn't have to involve lard...

Your design brief should be simple and concise, and allow you room for development. A design brief should not be a detailed description of what you intend to make — you can only say this after you've designed it and tried stuff out. Got that... describe the problem first. The rest comes later.

Research

Once you've written your design brief, you can start researching your project. This is what life is all about.

Research can help you get Ideas

It's worth doing your research carefully — it can give you loads of ideas for the rest of the design process. The point of doing research is to:

1) check that people will actually want your product (although you might have done this already when you chose your project).
2) find out what makes an existing product good or bad — talk to people who actually use this kind of product, and see what they like or dislike.
3) find out the materials, pre-manufactured components, techniques and ingredients that you can use, and how they will affect the manufacturing and selling costs.
4) give you a good starting point for designing.

There are Different Kinds of Research

You can do different kinds of research. These might include:

① Questionnaires — to find out people's likes/dislikes and so on. This will help you identify your target group and find out market trends (e.g. what things are becoming more popular).

② Disassembling a product (i.e. taking it apart) — this will help you find out how a current product is made and how it works. It could also give you information about different materials and processes used, and how existing products meet potential users' needs.

③ Measuring — to find out the weights and sizes of current products. This might give you an idea of the possible size, shape and weight of your product. You could also do some kind of sensory analysis (e.g. you could see how it tastes, feels, looks and smells).

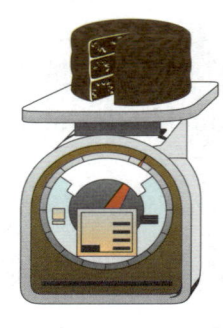

Research Analysis means Drawing Conclusions

Once you've done your research, you'll need to come to some conclusions. This means deciding how to use the information to help you with your design. This is called research analysis.

Try to do the following:

1) Pick out the useful information.
2) Explain what impact the research will have on your designs.
3) Suggest ways forward from the research gathered.

By the time you've done all this, you should have some ideas about how to tackle your project.

I disassembled my dog — he doesn't work any more...

Research is important. Trust me. More important at this stage than eating lard or melting chocolate. And one more thing while I'm ranting... you could also spend some time doing 'book research', e.g. finding out about any British or European standards your product will have to meet.

Section One — The Design Process

Design Specification

Once you've picked out the main points of your research, you're ready to put together a design specification. So put that lard away... you're not ready to do anything practical yet.

The Design Specification is a List of Conditions to Meet

The design specification describes the restrictions and possibilities of the product. It's a good point to start from when you get round to doing the more creative stuff.

1) The design specification gives certain conditions that the product will have to meet. Try to put your specification together in bullet form as specific points, rather than a paragraph of explanations.

> E.g. if your research tells you that people would never buy a lard cake weighing less than 400 grams, then your design specification might include the statement, "Must weigh more than 400 grams."

2) Once you've come up with a design, you need to compare it to the specification and confirm that each point is satisfied.

E.g. If your design specification contains these two points, then all of your designs should be at least 400 grams in weight and be dark brown on the outside.

> "The minimum weight will be 400 grams."
> "The product should be dark-brown on the outside."

3) Some points might be harder to compare to your specification simply by looking at the product.

> E.g. "The product should have a greasy texture."

For this, you'll need to get someone to test the product once it's been made/modelled.

4) Include points to describe some or all of the following:
   - a description of how it should look
   - details about what it has to do/be
   - materials, ingredients and baking methods
   - details of size/weight
   - safety points to consider
   - financial constraints

You might need to make More than One Specification

You'll probably need to produce several specifications as your project develops:

> Initial Design Specification — this is your first design specification. It should be done after your research analysis.

1) As you develop your design, you'll probably want to make some changes to your design specification. This is fine, as long as your design brief is being met and you have taken your research analysis into account.

2) Maybe as a result of some of your modelling (see page 5) you'll find that certain materials aren't suitable. You can add this information to an updated specification.

3) You can keep doing this until you end up with a final product specification.

I'd never buy a cake without lard in it...

If I told you that design specifications were going to get your pulse racing, you'd probably suspect I was lying. And of course, I would be lying. To be honest, they're a bit dull. But making a design specification is a vital step in designing and manufacturing a new product. So learn about it.

Section One — The Design Process

Generating Proposals

Now hold on to your hats, my wild young things — this is where it all starts to get a bit more interesting. This is the creative bit. This is where you start generating ideas.

There are a few Tricks that can help you Get Started

The following are suggestions to help you get started with designing:

1) Create a mood board — this is a load of different images, words, materials, colours and so on that might trigger ideas for your design.
2) Brainstorm — think up key words, questions and initial thoughts relating to your product. (Start off by just writing whatever ideas come into your head — analyse them later. *See p37.*)
3) Work from an existing product — but change some of its features or production methods so that it fits in with your specification.
4) Break the task up into smaller parts — design the 'look' of the product (aesthetics), then look at the technology involved and so on.

You need to Come up with a Range of Designs

1) You need to annotate (i.e. add notes to) your designs to fully explain your ideas. These notes could be about:

   - materials
   - shape
   - production method
   - sizes
   - cost
   - functions
   - user
   - advantages and disadvantages

2) You need to produce a wide range of appropriate solutions that you think could actually be made.

3) Try to use a range of techniques for presenting your designs. A good thing to do is to use different drawing techniques — for example:
   - perspective
   - orthographic projection
   - cross-sections
   - freehand sketching
   - digital camera photos
   - isometric projection

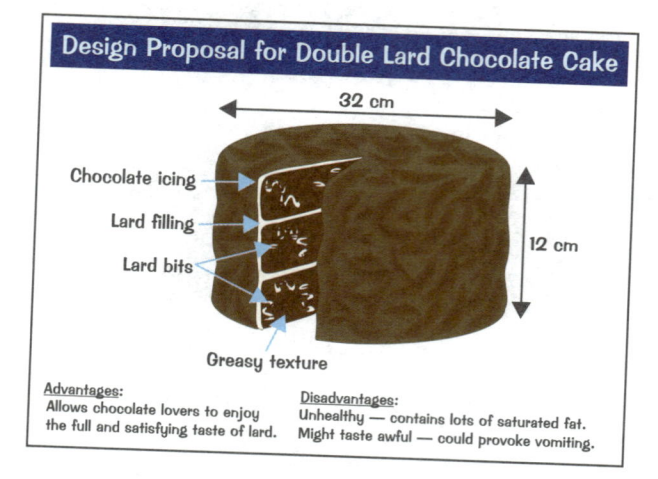

Design Proposal for Double Lard Chocolate Cake
- 32 cm wide, 12 cm tall
- Chocolate icing
- Lard filling
- Lard bits
- Greasy texture

Advantages: Allows chocolate lovers to enjoy the full and satisfying taste of lard.
Disadvantages: Unhealthy — contains lots of saturated fat. Might taste awful — could provoke vomiting.

4) Once you've got a few possible designs, you need to check that each one matches your specification — any that don't will not be suitable.

5) Finally, you need to choose one of your suitable designs to develop further.

Write whatever comes to mind — no hope for me then...

Think what someone will need to know to fully appreciate your design, and include this information on your proposal. And remember — you need to do quite a few of these so that you can choose the best one to develop and improve. This is the bit where you need to get your creative head on.

Section One — The Design Process

Development

Once you've decided on a design, you can begin to develop it further.
This is when your design should start to really take shape.

You can Develop your Design in Different Ways

Depending on the type of product that's being produced, further development might involve:

1) producing further sketches — but in more detail.
2) modelling and testing your idea. Or experimenting with different aspects of the design.
   E.g. you could try various materials, sizes and production methods.
3) using people's opinions about developments to help you arrive at a satisfactory solution.

Use lard instead of butter to make the cake mixture... ...to give an extra lardy taste.

Modelling means Trying Things Out

It can be useful to prototype or model your idea, especially if it's difficult to draw.

1) Try out different aspects of your design. If your design is quite large it may help to break it down into smaller, more manageable parts and test them individually.
2) Use a digital camera to record your models.
3) Evaluate the models (see next page), identifying reasons for selecting or rejecting different designs.

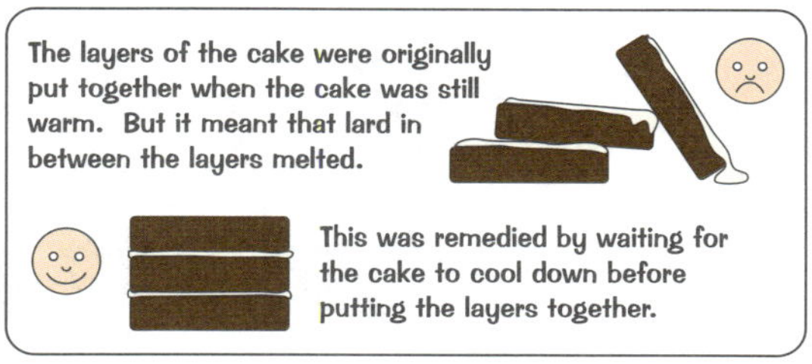

The layers of the cake were originally put together when the cake was still warm. But it meant that lard in between the layers melted.

This was remedied by waiting for the cake to cool down before putting the layers together.

This is a vital part of the design process. Ideally you should solve all the potential problems with your design at this stage.

Use the Results to Make Modifications

1) Results from your modelling and from your evaluation (see next page) will help you make important modifications (changes) to improve the product, and help it meet the design specification.
2) Suggested improvements could be:
   - ways to make the product itself better,
   - suggestions to make it more suitable for mass production.
3) But make sure you keep a record of whatever it is you find out (see next page).
4) Once you've made a modification to your design, you'll need to try it out to see if it actually improves things.
5) You might find that you end up modifying something, then trying it out, then making another modification and trying that out, then making another modification and trying that out, and so on. That's just the way it goes sometimes.

Modification — wear a parka and ride a scooter...

Modelling and evaluation *(see next page)* go hand in hand. It's pointless baking a cake and eating it if you're not going to bother learning anything from it. Ah, well... maybe not. If it's a really big cake.

Section One — The Design Process

Evaluation

Evaluation is an important part of any product development process,
and needs to be done at various stages along the way.

Keep Records of your Research and Testing

1) As you develop your product, keep records of any testing or market research you do. Write it all down, keep it, and refer back to it.

2) You might have tested materials for suitability, or tested components to see how well they work — but whatever you did, you need to write down all the results.

3) Compare the good and bad points of existing products with your model or prototype. Ask yourself if your product does the job better. Record your results.

4) Find out people's opinions and preferences about your models and prototypes (see previous page). This will help you to refine your ideas so you can arrive at the best solution.

5) Questionnaires help here — relevant market research questions might include:

> - Does the product work well?
> - Does the product work as well as similar products on the market?
> - Does the product look good? Is it well styled and modern-looking?
> - Are you unsure about any of the features? If so, which ones and why?
> - If this product were on the market, would you consider buying it?
> - If you were buying it, which price range do you think it would fall into?
> - Do you prefer another similar product to this one?

This type of evaluation is called formative evaluation — it's being used to help form the final design.

So would you consider buying one?

Get me a bucket...

Now You should Know Exactly what You're Making

By the time you've finished developing your ideas and have arrived at a final design, you should have found out / worked out:

1) The best materials, tools and other equipment to use (and their availability). This might include identifying any pre-manufactured components you're going to use.

2) The approximate manufacturing time needed to make each item.

3) How much it should cost to manufacture each item.

4) The most appropriate assembly process — this is going to be important information when it comes to planning production, and can be in the form of a flow chart (see page 8).

If you don't know what you're doing now, you never will...

At this stage of the process it should be crystal clear in your own mind how your final product should look, and how you're going to make it. But you're not finished yet. No, no, no, no, no... There's still the little business of actually making your pride and joy. Oh what fun... what fun...

Section One — The Design Process

Manufacturer's Specification

Now that you know <u>exactly</u> what you're going to make, you need to <u>communicate</u> all that info to the person that's actually going to <u>make</u> it.

You need to produce a Manufacturer's Specification

A manufacturer's specification can be a written <u>series of statements</u>, or <u>working drawings</u> and <u>sequence diagrams</u>. It has to explain <u>exactly</u> how the product will be made, and should include:

1) clear <u>construction</u> details explaining <u>exactly</u> how each bit's going to be made,
2) <u>sizes</u> — <u>precise measurements</u> of each part,
3) <u>tolerances</u> — the maximum and minimum sizes each part should be,
4) <u>finishing</u> details — any special sequences for finishing,
5) <u>quality control</u> instructions — where, when and how the manufacturing process should be checked. (See page 8 for time planning and page 45 for quality control.)
6) <u>costings</u> — how much each part costs, and details of any other costs involved.

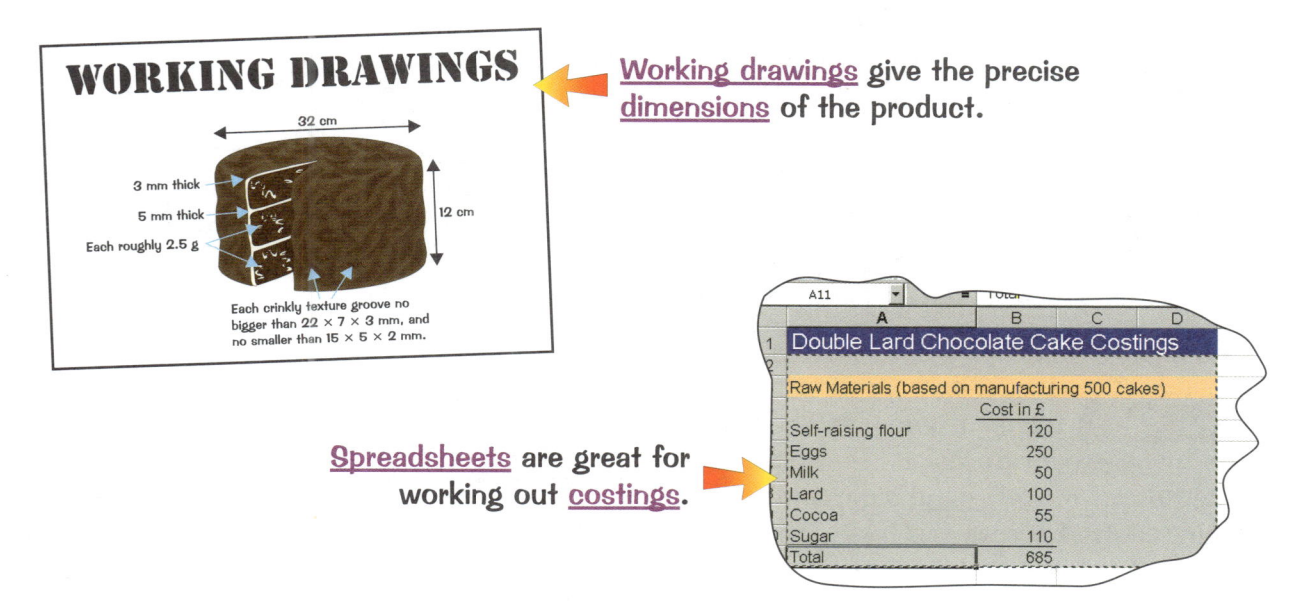

WORKING DRAWINGS

<u>Working drawings</u> give the precise <u>dimensions</u> of the product.

<u>Spreadsheets</u> are great for working out <u>costings</u>.

Plan how long the Production Process should take

When you get to this stage of product development, you also need to plan:

1) how your methods might have to <u>change</u> now you're producing the product <u>in volume</u>
2) <u>each stage</u> of the process in a great deal of <u>detail</u>
3) <u>how long</u> each stage will take
4) what needs to be <u>prepared</u> before you can start each stage
5) how you will <u>ensure consistency</u> and <u>quality</u>

See the <u>next page</u> as well for some different ways to help with this planning.

Manufacturer's specification — lard, lard and more lard...

You know what they say... the devil's in the detail. Yeah, well, I don't know exactly what that means, but it's probably got something to do with being really precise. And that's what you've got to do with your manufacturer's specification, or your masterpiece could end up as a dog's dinner.

Section One — The Design Process

Planning Production

Making one or two examples of your product is (relatively) easy.
But mass-producing it is a whole different ball game — and it takes a shed-load of careful planning.

Use Charts to help you

You need to work out how long each stage will take, and how these times will fit into the total time you've allowed for production. There are different ways of doing this:

① **Work Order** This can be produced as a table or flow chart. The purpose of a work order is to plan in sequence each task to be carried out. This will also include: tools and equipment, quality control stages, safety, and so on.

Start and end a flow chart with a sausage-shaped box.

Processes go in rectangular boxes.

Decisions go in diamond-shaped boxes. These let you show where quality should be checked.

② **Gantt Chart** This is a time plan showing the management of tasks. The tasks are listed down the left-hand side, and the timing plotted across the top. The coloured squares show how long each task takes, and the order they're done in.

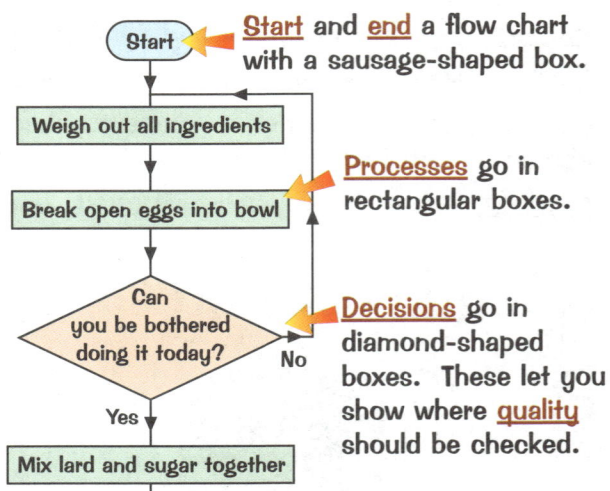

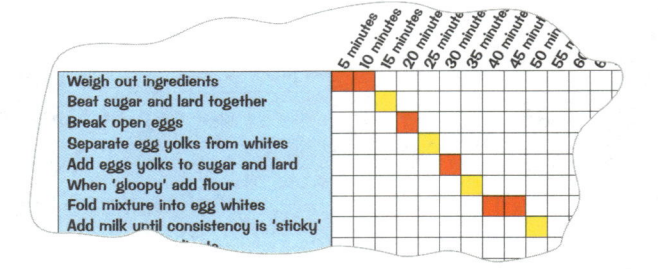

Test that the Product Works and Meets the Specification

1) When you think you've got the final product, it's vital to test it. Most important of all, you have to make sure it works, and meets the original design specification.

2) More questionnaires or surveys may help here. Ask a wide range of people to give their opinions about the finished product.

3) If your product fails to match any part of the specification, you must explain why. You really have to stand back and have a good hard think about your work. If you aren't satisfied with the way any part of the process went, think of how you could put it right for next time. Write it down in the form of a report.

4) This type of final evaluation is called summative evaluation — it summarises what you've learnt.

There's nothing like a good chart...

That's all you have to do then when it comes to your project. Just do in a few short weeks pretty much what it takes people in industry several months to complete, and you've got no worries.

Section One — The Design Process

Revision Summary for Section One

So that's the section over with, and what a roller-coaster ride full of fun and excitement it was. Yeah, well, the fun's not over yet, so don't look so disappointed. There's still some exciting revision questions for you to tackle. So try the questions, and then have a look back through the section to see if you got them all right. If you did — great. But if you got any wrong, have another careful read of the section and then <u>try the questions again</u>. And keep doing this until you can get all the questions right. That way, you know you're learning stuff.

1) What is the name given to the whole process of designing and making something?
2) Give three reasons why a new product might be needed.
3) Describe the kind of information you should put in your design brief.
4) Give three ways in which research can help you when you're designing a new product.
5) Explain how a questionnaire can be useful.
6) Give two other methods you could use to carry out research.
7) What is the name given to the process of drawing conclusions from your research?
8) Explain what is meant by a design specification.
9) Why might some points in a design specification be hard to assess just by looking at the product?
10) When would you compile an initial design specification?
11) Give three ways of getting started on your ideas.
12) What does the word 'annotate' mean?
13) What information should you include in your designs?
14) Why should you aim to produce a number of design ideas?
15) Give three techniques for presenting your designs.
16) Name two ways of developing your designs further.
17) Explain why it's useful to model your designs.
18) Describe two kinds of improvement you could make to your design.
19) When should you make an evaluation of your design? a) at the end of the project b) throughout the project c) evaluation is for wimps and sissies.
20) Describe two ways of evaluating your work.
21) What is meant by the phrase 'formative evaluation'?
22) Explain why a manufacturer's specification needs to be very precise.
23) Give four kinds of information that need to be on a manufacturer's specification.
24) When using a Gantt chart, what information goes down the left-hand side?
25) Describe two methods of planning how long the manufacturing process should take.
26) Describe the process of 'summative evaluation'.

Section One — The Design Process

Carbohydrates — Sugar

Carbohydrates are one of the biggest and most important food groups. Get your teeth into this...

Carbohydrates are Needed for Energy

Carbohydrates are split into three types:

SUGAR (MONOSACCHARIDE, DISACCHARIDE)
Includes simple sugars like glucose and fructose (monosaccharides), as well as double sugars (disaccharides) such as lactose and sucrose. They are easier to digest than polysaccharides.

STARCH (POLYSACCHARIDE)
Starch is a complex sugar. It needs to be broken down by digestion before the energy can be used. That's why it's good to eat starchy foods like pasta and rice a few hours before playing loads of sport.

NSP (NON-STARCH POLYSACCHARIDES)
NSPs are things like fibre and bulk. Bran, fruit, beans and brown bread contain lots of fibre.

Carbohydrates are good sources of energy. But energy that isn't used is stored by the body as fat. So it's often carbohydrates, not fats, that make people fat.

There are Several Types of Sugar Used in Home Baking

1) Granulated — for general kitchen use. Used to sweeten tea and sprinkle on breakfast cereal.
2) Caster sugar — this has finer crystals than granulated and is used for baking, especially cakes and biscuits, which require a fine texture.
3) Brown sugars — demerara and muscovado are brown sugars with strong distinctive flavours. These are used in rich fruit cakes, gingerbread and Christmas puddings.
4) Icing sugar is a fine, white, powdery sugar used for icings and confectionery.

Sugar substitutes can be used to sweeten things like drinks. They're better for your teeth than sugar and contain far fewer calories, so they're good for people who are on a slimming diet. They're also good for diabetics who have to control their sugar intake. Sugar substitutes are unsuitable for home baking as they don't have the same properties as cane sugar.

Sugar is Used Almost Everywhere in Food Manufacturing

Sugar is used widely in food manufacturing (you'd be surprised how many savoury products contain sugar). It is found in a variety of disguises on the ingredients label: fructose, dextrose, sucrose, inverted sugar, maltose, lactose and glucose are all sugars.

My god! This stuff's everywhere... Help me somebody... help!

Sugar is used in loads of products, such as:
1) Jam — sugar acts as a preservative, gives texture and volume and helps the jam set.
2) Creamed mixtures (such as in baking cakes) — Sugar is beaten with fat to incorporate air, which helps lighten the cakes.
3) Bread — Sugar speeds up fermentation.
4) Cakes, biscuits and pastries — to add sweetness and colour, prevent drying out and give texture and volume.

My Nan bakes my cakes — she uses grannylated sugar...

Sugar is obviously good in some ways — it tastes great, and you get sweets, cakes, biscuits, chocolates and all things good from it. But it rots your teeth. Though I don't miss mine *that* much.

Carbohydrates — Starch

Starch has a ton of uses. Well actually about a page's worth...

Starch is Really Useful for Making Food Products

Because of starch's properties and working characteristics
it's used as a bulking agent, a gelling agent and a thickening agent:

STARCH IS USED AS A BULKING AGENT

Starch granules swell when a liquid is added and this forms the bulk in the product. The starch can form the main structure of the product and so provides the bulk.

STARCH IS USED AS A GELLING AGENT

When moisture is added to starch granules and heat is applied:
1) Starch granules begin to absorb the liquid and swell.
2) At 80°C the starch particles break open, making the mixture thick and viscous. This is GELATINISATION.
3) Gelatinisation is completed when the liquid reaches 100°C.
4) The thickened liquid now forms a GEL.
5) On cooling the gel solidifies and takes the form of the container it's in.

STARCH IS USED AS A THICKENING AGENT

Sauces and gravies are often made using starch (flour) and liquid.
The degree of thickness depends on the amount of starch and liquid.
1) The starch and liquid are mixed together.
2) The starch particles form a SUSPENSION — they don't dissolve.
3) The mixture is stirred to keep the particles suspended.
4) Heat is applied and GELATINISATION occurs.

STARCH IS USED IN MANUFACTURED PRODUCTS

Modified starch (see below) is used to thicken things like instant desserts, whipped cream, yoghurts and packet soup. Usually a liquid is added to the starch and it is stirred or whisked.

Modified Starches are Called Smart Starches

Modified starches are those which have been altered to react to different environments.
In food technology we refer to them as smart starches.

1) Pre-gelatinised starch thickens instantly when mixed with hot water (e.g. packet custard, pot noodles).
2) When protein is heated it can coagulate and squeeze out the fat and water. This is called syneresis. Some starches allow products to be reheated with no syneresis. This is useful in dishes which are cooked from frozen (e.g. lasagne).
3) Some modified starches aren't affected by acid, so they can be used to thicken products (e.g. low calorie salad cream — which contains vinegar).

I love starch too — more than I love eating my toenails...

Interesting starch fact (#1 in a series of 1): modified starch from barley has similar properties to fat and could be used to make stuff like low fat cake or biscuits. Hmm — but where's the fun in that...

Carbohydrates — Cereals and Flour

Eating grass should mainly be left to cows and sheep, but certain members of the grass family are grown for food (the seeds, not the blades of grass) — these are called cereals.

Cereals are used for Everything, Everywhere

Cereals contain lots of carbohydrates and are often used for their starchy properties.

They can be prepared in a variety of ways and used as part of a basic diet.

Wheat, oats, barley and rye are the main cereals grown in temperate climates. Rice, maize and millet are the main ones grown in tropical lands.

Flour can be made from Most Cereals

Flour is made up into various products, which form the staple diet for people in many countries:
1) Bread, cakes and biscuits across the western world are made with flour from wheat.
2) Italians use durum wheat to make pasta and cornmeal from maize to make polenta.
3) South Americans use cornmeal from maize to make cornbread.
4) Oatmeal is traditionally used in Scotland to produce biscuits and cakes as well as porridge.
5) Bread made from rye is eaten by people in Northern Europe.
6) Rice flour made from rice is often used in cakes.

Cereals can also be used as part of a meal, like couscous with vegetable stew, or rice with curry (or whatever).

Wheat can be Strong or Soft

'Strong' Flour is Used to Make Bread

'Strong' wheat is grown in countries with hot summers and very cold winters — such as Canada. Strong white flour has loads of a protein called gluten in it. When gluten is mixed with a liquid, it becomes stretchy and elastic. This helps the bread to rise and stretch during making and baking. Using wholemeal flour can produce a loaf with a denser, closer texture because the bran and wheatgerm it contains weaken the gluten and prevent it from working properly.
This problem can be overcome by using a mixture of strong white and strong wholemeal flour.

'Soft' Flour is Used to Make Cakes

'Soft' flour is made from wheat grown in countries with long summers and short winters — such as the Mediterranean countries. 'Soft' flour is more suitable for cake-making because it has a low gluten content and produces a cake with a soft tender crumb. Lovely.
Self-raising flour is often used because it has a controlled amount of raising agent so you know exactly what you're getting. Unlike Geoff here…

I could murder some cornflakes — I'm a cereal killer…

Before you started this page you may have thought that cereals weren't that exciting really — but how wrong you were. For example, I'll bet you didn't realise that flour could be strong. Still I don't care what anyone says, I'd rather fight the world's strongest flour than a hungry sumo wrestler.

Section Two — Materials and Components

Carbohydrates — Wheat

Wheat is the cereal most commonly used in food technology, so it's got a page all to itself...

The Wheat Grain is Made Up of Three Important Parts

1) Bran — the outside coat of the wheat, which provides dietary fibre.

2) Wheatgerm — a very small part of the wheat grain, but provides vitamins and oils.

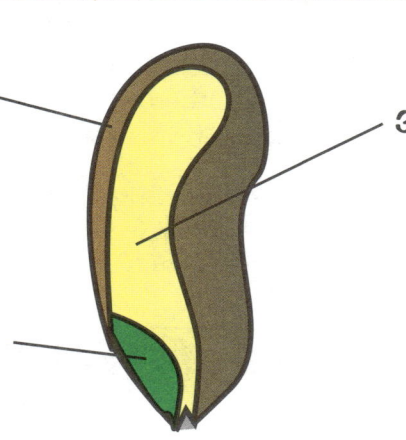

3) Endosperm — this forms the main part of the wheat grain (85%). It is the white starchy part of the grain and provides protein and carbohydrate.

Wheat is Turned Into Flour by Milling

To get from wheat to flour, the wheat is:

1) cleaned: the wheat is sieved, rubbed clean and passed through a process which removes any unwanted parts. It's then washed.
2) conditioned: the wheat is dried or moistened to prepare it for milling.
3) milled: the grains are passed through a series of rollers which break them down so that the endosperm (white starchy inside part) can be scraped away from the bran (outer coat).
4) further milled and sieved: continues until the correct grade of white flour is produced.
5) mixed: this can create different flours. These flours can vary in texture and type.
6) sterilised and packaged: to ensure that the flour reaches the consumer in good condition.

Different Kinds of Milling Produce Different Flours

The flavour, texture and colour of the flour is influenced by the process of milling the wheat. Stainless steel rollers are mainly used for grinding the wheat.

1) Stone rollers (grinders) produce stoneground flour (which has a coarser texture).
2) Wholemeal flour is made by grinding the whole of the wheat, including the outer (bran) layer. This flour also has a coarser texture as well as a darker colour and 'nutty' flavour.
3) White flour is made by using just the inner starchy part of the grain (endosperm).
4) Self-raising flour is made by adding raising agents to the flour during processing.
5) Improved technology has led to other flours (e.g. granary and soft-sponge flour).

Wholemeal bread. (Nice and soft. Just waiting to be stuck in the toaster then smothered in butter. Mmmmmmm....)

I thought I'd write a gag — but then I thought, wheat's the point?...

Make sure you know how wheat is turned into flour. Learn the six main points first, then learn the details for each point. Then write everything down from memory. And then have a cup of tea.

Section Two — Materials and Components

Proteins — Meat

Meat, poultry and fish are important because they provide high-grade protein and other essential nutrients. But bacteria also like them, so you have to be really careful when buying, storing, preparing or cooking them. If you're not, you can end up with the runs, or something even worse.

Protein is Needed for Growth and Repair

1) Protein is broken down by the body into amino acids. These are then made into new proteins.
2) The body can make some proteins, but not others — you have to eat them.
3) These are called the Essential Amino Acids and there are eight of them for adults (ten for children).

High Biological Value (HBV) proteins contain all ten, e.g. meat, fish, eggs, milk and soya beans.
Low Biological Value (LBV) proteins don't contain all ten e.g. cereals, pulses and nuts.
(Note: you can still get all the essential amino acids from LBV proteins as long as you eat a variety regularly)

There are Three Main Types of Meat Eaten in the UK...

Beef   Pork    Lamb

Products and dishes made from these meats include: beefburgers, sausages, pies, chilli con carne, spaghetti Bolognese, shepherd's pie and spam. And there are loads more...

...Three Main Types of Poultry...

Many people have stopped eating red meat and turned to the poultry. This is partly due to the 'bad press' for meat including BSE in the 1990s and the foot-and-mouth outbreak of 2001.

The three main types of poultry eaten in the UK are:

Chicken   Turkey    Duck

SALMONELLA
Poultry, especially chicken, is very susceptible to the food poisoning bacteria salmonella. So it's essential to take precautions at every stage — from purchase to storage, preparation, cooking and serving.

Poultry, and chicken in particular, can be cooked and made into many products (e.g. chicken Kiev, burgers, Kentucky and Maryland chicken). There's also a wide range of chicken cuts such as drumsticks, breast and wings.

What do you call a cat who swallowed a duck?...

Sure, meat's got protein in it, but it contains other stuff as well — e.g. red meat has loads of iron, and liver has loads of vitamins. But meat also has lots and lots of saturated fat. Shame.

Section Two — Materials and Components

Proteins — Fish and Alternatives

...and Three Main Types of Fish...

Oily fish: e.g. herring, mackerel, salmon, tuna.

Shellfish: e.g. crab, lobster, mussels.

White fish: e.g. cod, haddock, plaice, skate.

Salmon

Lobster

Cod (but not him, his name's Gordon Caine).

Honestly, I'm not trying to get you drunk.

My name's Gordon Caine, and this is my favourite cod.

Fish is highly nutritious — it contains loads of vitamins, plus omega 3 oils that are dead good for you. Seafood is used in loads of manufactured products, such as fish fingers, fish cakes, fisherman's pie, crabsticks and scampi.
Prawn cocktail, fish kedgeree and cod mornay are well known fish dishes that are easy to make.

There are Now Loads of Meat Replacements

1) For a variety of reasons, more and more people are becoming vegetarian in the UK. It's important that they have a healthy diet with the essential proteins and nutrients.

2) There are many alternatives to meat — these foods are often called alternative proteins — these include: Tofu — made from soya beans.
   TVP (Textured Vegetable Protein) — also made from soya beans.
   Quorn — made from a mushroom-like fungus and egg white.

3) These products can be put together in a variety of ways to resemble meat or chicken:
   TVP can be made into sausages, burgers and ready meals.
   Tofu is usually just stir-fried, but it can also be used in desserts.
   Quorn is more often used where you'd normally use chicken, and is available as chunks (e.g. for stir fries), mince (e.g. for chilli con carne) or fillets (e.g. to serve in sauces).

   spot the difference...

4) These meat replacements usually don't taste of much, so they're often flavoured. One way of doing this is by marinating them (soaking them in a mixture of oil, wine, vinegar and herbs and things) before cooking — so they absorb the flavour of the marinade.

...a duck-filled-fatty-puss...

Hardly anyone considers the rights of a meat substitute, do they... but I do. When I'm tucking into my tasty-sounding TVP-burger, I often wonder about baby TVPs running around their vegetable patch, and then being snatched away from mummy TVP to be made into food. Makes me cry.

Section Two — Materials and Components

Vitamins and Minerals

Vitamins and minerals are essential for a healthy body. They help other nutrients to work and can prevent certain diseases. That's why your Mum makes you eat spinach...

We need a Balance of Different Vitamins and Minerals

Vitamin A
1) We get most of our vitamin A from retinol which can be found in liver, butter, fish oils and eggs.
2) We can also make it from carotene, which is found in orange or yellow fruit & veg and margarine.
3) Vitamin A is needed for good eyesight (especially night vision) and growth and functions of tissues.

Vitamin B Group
1) Found in cereals, liver, kidney, yeast, peas, pulses, dairy produce, meat and fish.
2) B(1) thiamin: helps with the nervous system and the release of energy from carbohydrates.
3) B(2) riboflavin: helps with the release of energy as well as repair and maintenance of tissues.
4) Niacin: helps with the release of energy as it forms part of the enzymes needed.
5) Folic acid: this is crucial for growth and is particularly important for women planning pregnancy, as low levels of folate at conception can increase the risk of a baby being born with spina bifida.

Vitamin C (also known as Ascorbic Acid)
1) Found in citrus fruits (lemons, oranges etc), green vegetables, peppers and potatoes.
2) Good for protecting the body from infection and allergies, helps in the absorption of calcium and iron from food and helps to maintain the walls of the blood vessels and heal wounds.

Vitamin D (also known as Calciferol)
1) Found in fatty fish and eggs and is produced in the body when the skin is exposed to sunlight.
2) Good for aiding the absorption of calcium for strong bones and teeth.

Calcium
1) Found in milk products, tofu, salmon, green leafy vegetables, hard water and white bread.
2) Needed for strong bones and teeth and the correct working of the nerves and muscles.
3) Growing children need calcium every day for strong bones and teeth. Lack of calcium in youth can lead to problems in later life (e.g. osteoporosis).

Iron
1) Found in dark green vegetables (e.g. spinach) and meat (especially liver and kidney).
2) Needed to form part of the haemoglobin which gives blood cells their red colour. Lack of iron causes a deficiency disease called anaemia.

Fruit and Vegetables are Dead Healthy

In a normal healthy diet, fruit and vegetables give you:
1) The majority of your vitamin C intake (about 90%).
2) Dietary fibre and bulk (also known as NSP — non-starch polysaccharides).
3) Vitamins A and B (see above).
4) Iron and calcium (see above).
5) Not much fat (except avocados).
6) Loads of water.
7) Small amounts of protein.

Vitamin B Group? — oh yeah, my dad's got one of their records...

Loads and loads of info. And just in case you were wondering, yes, you do need to learn it all.

Section Two — Materials and Components

Fruit and Vegetables

For good health the Government recommends we eat 5 portions of fruit and veg per day. These portions could be dried, fresh, tinned or frozen. Fruit juice counts (yay) — but potatoes don't (boo).

Fruit and Vegetables have a Variety of Sensory Properties

Fruit and vegetables contain loads of nutrients. But they also make meals taste better. They add:

1) Colour to meals — e.g. peas, sweetcorn, etc.
2) Texture — e.g. crunchy carrots.
3) Flavour — e.g. onions in meat dishes.
4) Contrast to a meal — e.g. apple sauce with roast pork.
5) Decoration or garnish to meals — e.g. side salad.

They can make a refreshing finish to a meal (e.g. a fruit salad) as well as an easy-to-eat snack.

Prepare Fruit and Veg Carefully to Keep the Good Stuff

The nutrients, flavour and colour of vegetables can be easily lost or spoilt through overcooking and poor storage. Here's how to avoid that happening:

1) Store fruit and vegetables in a cool and dark place for a short period of time.
2) Prepare fruit and vegetables JUST before you need them — vitamin C, in particular, starts to go once the fruit and vegetables are picked, stored, cut or peeled.
3) Don't chop fruit and vegetables into small pieces — it exposes more of the surface and more nutrients are lost.
4) Don't leave vegetables to stand in water — vitamins B and C dissolve away into the water.
5) Most of the nutrients and the fibre (NSP) are found just below the skin of fruit and vegetables, so peel very thinly or use them cleaned and unpeeled if possible (like jacket potatoes).
6) Fruit and vegetables should be cooked as quickly as possible in a small amount of water. Steaming or microwaving them are the best ways to keep the nutrients.

Mucho Vitamins B and C.

Bananas need to be stored separately... they give off a gas which makes other fruit and vegetables ripen quickly and spoil.

There are Eight Types of Vegetable

There is an increasing variety of vegetables available — like organic stuff, as well as new things like baby vegetables. But veg can still be classified under the following headings:

1) Tubers — e.g. potatoes, yams, Jerusalem artichokes, sweet potatoes
2) Leaves — e.g. cabbage, sprouts, spinach, lettuce, watercress, kale
3) Roots — e.g. carrots, parsnips, radishes, cassava, swede, turnip
4) Flowers / flower heads — e.g. cauliflower, broccoli
5) Pods and seeds — e.g. beans, sweetcorn, peas, mangetout, okra
6) Stems — e.g. celery, asparagus
7) Bulbs — e.g. fennel, onions, leeks, shallots, spring onions
8) Fruits — e.g. tomatoes, cucumbers, peppers, aubergines, avocados, marrows, courgettes, chillies

That's the end of the page on veg — yep, that's shallot...

Umm... I can't actually think of anything else useful to say. So I'll keep my mouth shut for once.

Section Two — Materials and Components

Fats and Oils

Fats and oils get a lot of bad press — everyone's always telling you to cut down on fat. That's probably good advice, but don't go believing that they're all bad.

There are Six Main Types of Fats and Oils

1) Butter is made from churning cream.
2) Margarine is blended from vegetable oils. *This is done using a process called hydrogenation, which makes them solid at room temperature.*
3) Lard is made from pig fat.
4) Suet is made from the fat which protects animals' vital organs.
5) Oils are extracted from pressed seeds (e.g. rape seed, sunflower seed, soya bean).
6) Low-fat spreads are emulsions of vegetable oils *(usually hydrogenated — see note above)* and water.

Fats and Oils have Loads of Uses

1) Cooking — deep frying (e.g. fish and chips) and shallow frying (e.g. eggs).
2) Greasing — to stop cakes, biscuits and the like sticking to baking tins.
3) Adding colour — butter in pastry makes it golden yellow.
4) Adding flavour — butter in shortbread and pastry make them taste fantastic.
5) Adding air (in cake-making) — when fat is creamed with sugar it helps trap air.
6) Enriching — makes sauces taste better.
7) Shortening (in pastry and biscuits) — rubbing fat into flour prevents gluten sticking and makes products 'short' — so they're a bit crumbly.
8) Moistening and forming a waterproof barrier — e.g. butter on bread when making sandwiches. Many manufactured products have fat in to help retain moisture and prevent them going stale.

Lionel wasn't convinced about using fat to keep warm.

Fats have Some Nutritional Value

1) Fats supply a concentrated source of energy.
2) Fatty foods provide a source of the fat-soluble vitamins A, D, E and K.
3) Fats provide certain fatty acids which are essential to the structure and function of body cells.

Unsaturated Fats OK — Saturated Fats Bad

Our bodies use fat to make cholesterol, which is an essential part of all cell membranes and is needed to make hormones.
But, scientists think that too much cholesterol in the diet can increase the risk of heart disease — and that to reduce that risk we should eat less saturated fat.

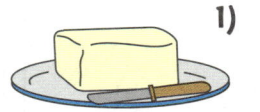

1) Saturated fats — come mainly from animal sources (e.g. meat, butter, suet, dripping, lard) and are solid or semi-solid at room temperature. *(And as I said, they're often associated with high amounts of cholesterol.)*

2) Unsaturated fats — come mainly from vegetable sources (e.g. vegetable oils) and are usually liquid at room temperature. The main oils used in cooking are peanut, sunflower, corn, soya, rapeseed and olive oil.

Lard... suet... dripping... Mmmm... that sounds real good...

Processed foods can contain *loads* of fat, so it's worth checking out the alternatives. Fresh veg is great, although memories of those bullet-like sprouts you get given as a kid can put you off a bit.

Section Two — Materials and Components

Dairy Products

Milk's ace. It contains nearly all the essential nutrients — protein, fat, carbohydrate, phosphorus, calcium and vitamins A, D and B12. And it can be processed to make things like cheese and butter.

You can Buy Milk in Various Different Forms

There are three different types of milk...
1) Whole milk has 3.5% fat.
2) Skimmed milk has nearly all the fat removed (only 0.1% left) and looks less white and creamy.
3) Semi-skimmed milk has about half the fat of whole milk, but tastes reasonably similar.

1) Milk is often homogenised to evenly distribute the fat and stop the cream floating to the top.

   Homogenisation: milk forced through tiny holes — breaking down the fat into fine globules, which remain evenly distributed

2) Most milk you buy is also pasteurised to kill any harmful bacteria and make the milk last longer.

   Pasteurisation: heating the milk to 72°C and holding the temperature for 16 seconds

3) UHT (ultra heat-treated) milk, also known as long-life milk, is taken to a very high temperature, to kill all the bacteria. UHT milk can be kept for months — but it's got a bit of a funny taste.

   UHT: milk is heated to 132-140°C for one second, rapidly cooled and then packaged

4) Milk can also be dried. It's handy to have in the store cupboard as it'll keep for several months. It's powdered, and you add water. But it really doesn't taste that great.

Secondary Processing of Milk Creates Other Products

1) **CREAM**: if (non-homogenised) milk is left to stand, the cream rises to the top, and you can skim it off. Different types of cream are made by taking different amounts of cream off in different ways:
   - Single cream — low fat content and doesn't thicken if beaten,
   - Double cream — thick with a high fat content,
   - Whipping cream — contains just enough butterfat so it can be whipped until stiff.

   Cream can be processed further to create clotted cream, sour cream, sterilised cream, ice cream, aerosol cream, and creme fraiche.

2) **BUTTER**: is made by churning (stirring) cream. After a while, the cream starts to solidify and turn into butter. Sometimes butter is salted to add flavour.

3) **YOGHURT**: is made by adding bacteria to milk (usually *lactobacillus acidophilus* & *streptococcus thermophilus*). Different types of bacteria and additives produce different yoghurts, like natural, fruit-flavoured, thick and creamy, bio, Greek-style, low fat and set.

4) **CHEESE**: if milk stands for several days, it sours and separates into curd (which is thick) and the whey (which is watery). This separation process is often speeded up using rennet (a protein from a calf's stomach). The whey is drained off and the curd is pressed to remove more whey, and shaped. Flavourings are sometimes added (e.g. salt, chives) at this stage. It's then left to mature for a few months — then it's cheese.
   Cheeses are categorised according to their fat content and hardness.

   When cheese is heated it changes colour, becoming golden brown. And the flavour changes too. If cooking continues the fat melts and separates out, and the protein coagulates — it shrinks and separates from the fat and the water. This is bad — the cheese becomes tough and stringy, which makes it difficult to digest, and generally a bit nasty.

   this is cheese

I like cheese from the 80s — Duran Duran, Wham, Aha...

I told you milk was pretty great. Only snag is, cos there's loads of types of milk, plus a load of other products made from milk, there's quite a few things to learn — but that's life, so get learnin'.

Section Two — Materials and Components

Eggs

We mainly eat hens' eggs, but goose, duck and quail eggs are also popular with some people. Anyway eggs is eggs and they're great.

NUTRITIONAL CONTENT OF EGGS
protein, fat (mainly saturated), vitamin A,
minerals: iron, calcium, phosphorus.

Eggs have Loads of Uses and Functions in Cooking

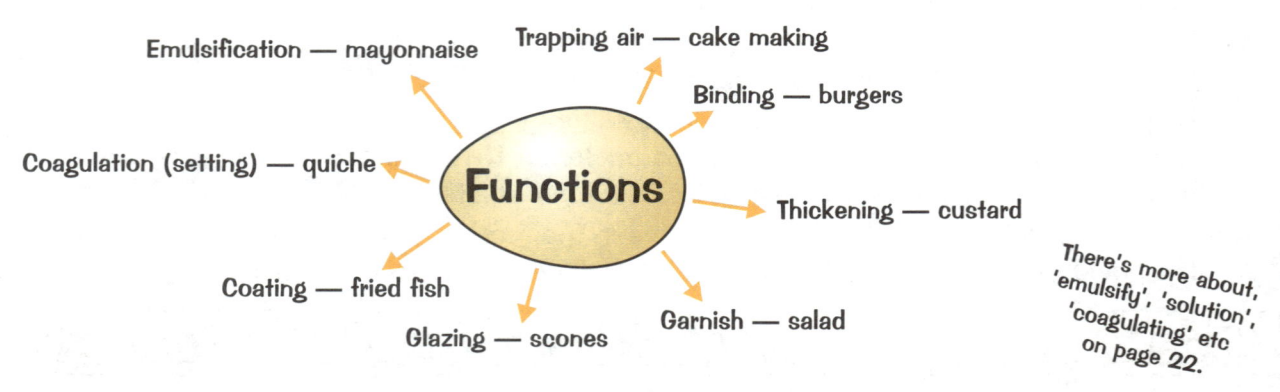

Functions:
- Emulsification — mayonnaise
- Trapping air — cake making
- Binding — burgers
- Coagulation (setting) — quiche
- Thickening — custard
- Coating — fried fish
- Garnish — salad
- Glazing — scones

There's more about 'emulsify', 'solution', 'coagulating' etc on page 22.

1) **Aeration** — egg white entraps air when it is beaten — because the protein stretches.
2) **Emulsification** — oil and water mixed together will form an emulsion. But usually they will only stay in suspension for a short while. Lecithin found in egg yolks acts to keep the emulsion stable.
3) **Thickening** — egg white coagulates at 60°C and yolk at 70°C, so when these temperatures are reached it sets and stays 'thickened' (like in custard or quiche mixture).
4) **Binding** — coagulation sticks the ingredients together as they cook.
5) **Glazing** (for pastry, etc) — during baking, the egg glaze turns golden brown.
6) **Coating** — foods are brushed with egg and then dipped in breadcrumbs. During cooking, the egg coagulates (again) forming a strong 'jacket'. This holds the product together and prevents oil from being absorbed during frying.

Eggs May Contain Salmonella

1) Raw eggs may contain the bacteria salmonella — which causes severe food poisoning.
2) It's **VERY IMPORTANT** that eggs are cooked thoroughly so that all bacteria are destroyed.
3) You should be extra careful when cooking eggs which are to be eaten by pregnant women, babies and elderly or frail people.
4) Manufacturers often use dried or pasteurised egg to be on the safe side, like for mayonnaise.

Would you like a duck egg for tea? Only if you 'quack' it for me...

Eggs are used left, right and centre in cooking so keep going over that list of the uses and functions. But remember — they can carry salmonella, so watch out.

Section Two — Materials and Components

Revision Summary for Section Two

Another section rattles to an end and I know you'll be eager to get on to Section Three. But hold your horses just one second — before you go racing on, check you've remembered all the stuff in this section. You know what to do — yep, only one way to find out what you've learnt — go over these questions, look back at any you aren't sure about, and then do the questions again. Keep going until it's easier than an omelette. Well, what are you waiting for — Section Three beckons...

1) Name the three types of carbohydrate and give an example of each.
2) Name one use for brown sugar, other than putting it in your coffee.
3) What's the main function of sugar in jam-making?
4) Describe what happens to starch when it is heated in a liquid. What is this process called?
5) Name one modified starch and an example of how it's used.
6) Name two cereals that are grown in temperate climates and two that are grown in tropical climates.
7) Name three cereals that are served as accompaniments with meals.
8) Name three different types of wheat flour and explain how each is used in cooking.
9) Draw a diagram of a wheat grain. Label the main parts and write down what nutrients each part contains.
10) List in order the processes involved in milling wheat. (You could draw a flowchart if you like.)
11) Why do our bodies need protein?
12) What are 'HBV proteins' and 'LBV proteins'?
13) Why is it important to thoroughly cook poultry? Is it:
    a) to avoid food poisoning OR   b) to stop the poultry running away before you eat it.
14) Name the three main categories of fish.
15) Name three 'alternative proteins' and describe one way you could add flavour to them.
16) For each of the following vitamins and minerals, write down
    a) why our bodies need it, and b) two good sources of it:
    vitamin A, thiamin, riboflavin, niacin, folic acid, ascorbic acid, califerol, calcium, iron
17) Why is it important to eat 5 portions of fruit and vegetables a day?
18) How can you reduce the loss of nutrients when preparing and cooking vegetables?
19) Describe four different fats.
20) Give the functions of fat in: a) shortcrust pastry, b) victoria sandwich cake, c) shortbread.
21) Why is fat important in the diet?
22) Give two differences between saturated and polyunsaturated fat.
23) Name three types of milk (milkshake doesn't count).
24) Which of these products isn't made from milk?
    a) cheese b) cream c) bacon, eggs and black pudding with fried mushrooms and beans.
25) Why are dairy products considered 'high risk' foods?
26) What happens to cheese when it is heated?
27) What is the nutritional value of an egg?
28) Give three uses for eggs.
29) What function do eggs have in cake-making?
30) What food poisoning bacteria are associated with eggs (and chickens)?

SECTION THREE — FOOD PROCESSES

Combining Ingredients

How a product turns out depends not only on the type and amount of ingredients but also on how they react with each other.

Solution — Ingredients Added to a Liquid

1) This is one of the simplest types of mixture.
2) It's formed if the ingredients dissolve into the liquid becoming homogeneous (uniform).

Emulsion — Oil and Watery Stuff Mixed Together

1) Oil and watery ingredients will not stay mixed together (you have to keep shaking or stirring it all the time), unless you use an emulsifier.
2) Emulsifiers keep the oil suspended throughout the liquid.
3) Egg yolk contains an emulsifier called Lecithin.
4) Manufacturers have to use emulsifiers in creamed cake mixtures, butter, margarine, chocolate, mayonnaise, salad cream and any other product which contains both oil and a watery liquid.

mayonnaise — the ultimate emulsion

Suspensions — a Solid Held in a Liquid

1) In a suspension the solid will not dissolve and may sink if the mixture is not stirred, e.g. packet soup in cold water.
2) However, starchy suspensions can be prevented from separating by heating, which causes gelatinisation (see p11).

Gels — a Small Amount of Solid Sets a Lot of Liquid

1) A gel is like a thick solution.
   (Well... not exactly, but the full chemistryish explanation gets a bit complicated.)
2) The liquid is often referred to as 'set' but it's quite soft (e.g. jam).
3) Pectin, when mixed with acid (from the fruit) and sugar, helps jams and jellies set.

Foams — Air Mixed with a Liquid

1) A good example is meringue, where air is whisked into egg white.
2) Sugar can stabilise the foam (stop it changing and separating).
3) Heating will coagulate (semi-solidify) the protein and set the foam (meringue).
4) Double cream and whipping cream can be whisked to incorporate air to form a foam, which can then be piped.

We need to find a solution soon — I can't take the suspension...

A lot of food processes are all about combining different foods. The reactions you get when you do this are the key to lots of different products — jam wouldn't be jam if it didn't form a gel and whipped cream wouldn't be half the fun if it wasn't a foam.

Different Types of Production

Industry uses different production methods, depending on the type and number of items to be made.

Try it out with a Small Scale Prototype

1) People in the food industry develop a prototype and try it out to see if it would sell.
2) Likewise in your coursework you go through the process of developing a food product until you have one that you're happy with and can show would be successful if it was manufactured.

Jobbing Production — Making a One-Off Product

1) This is where you're making a single product.
2) Every item made will be different, to meet the customer's individual and specific requirements, e.g. a wedding or birthday cake.
3) It needs an individual recipe and method.
4) It will probably require specialised skills from experienced workers.
5) It takes more time and is more labour-intensive than other production methods.
6) It makes for a high quality product, but normally at a high cost.

Batch Production — A Specified Quantity of a Product

1) This is for making a specific quantity of a product on a large or small scale (50-5000). 
2) Batches can be repeated as many times as required.
3) The machinery and labour used need to be flexible, so they can quickly change from making one batch to making another batch of a similar product.
4) The time between batches, when machines have to be cleaned or changed around, is called down time. This is unproductive and needs to be kept as short as possible so the manufacturer doesn't lose money.

Continuous Production — Non-Stop Production 24hrs/day

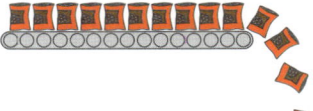

1) This involves non-stop, uninterrupted production.
2) It's used for products which are sold regularly and in large numbers (e.g. baked beans).
3) The specialised equipment required is very expensive, so it would cost too much to turn it off. It has to keep running and producing continuously.
4) If anything goes wrong, it can take time to get it going again — and time means money.

Computer-Aided Manufacture (CAM) Makes it Quicker

1) This is where large sections, or the whole production, are controlled by computers. Anything from bread-making machines to computerised scales can be used (see p28-29).
2) It is very fast and requires fewer workers — therefore lowering production costs.
3) The quality of the product is very high.
4) It is very hygienic as the food is not handled.
5) It is safer for the workers, as all the tasks are carried out by machine.

We want Labour to be flexible? — no problem there then...

Using machines and making things in huge numbers makes the whole process quicker and therefore makes the products cheaper. Still, sometimes it's worth splashing out a bit of extra money on something which has had that bit more time spent on it — like a CGP book. Quite.

Section Three — Food Processes

Food Contamination and Bacteria

Food manufacturers have to produce food that's safe to eat. When you're buying, preparing, cooking, serving or storing food, you also need to make sure it's done in the safest way possible.

Bacteria are the Main Source of Food Poisoning

1) Bacteria are single-celled organisms. They're the main source of food poisoning and are found in air, water, soil, people, animals — pretty much everywhere really.
2) They can only be seen under a microscope.
3) They often don't make the food look, taste or smell any different.
4) With the right conditions (e.g. food, warmth, moisture and time) they can multiply very rapidly.
5) Food poisoning symptoms include sickness, diarrhoea, stomach cramps and fever. In extreme cases, especially where people are old or vulnerable, it can result in death.

There are Certain High-Risk Foods

Bacteria really like foods which are moist and high in protein.
High-risk foods include:
1) meat, fish and poultry
2) dairy products and eggs
3) gravies, stocks and sauces
4) shellfish and other seafood
5) cooked rice

Take Some Simple Steps to Avoid Cross-Contamination

When working with food you must be very careful not to pass bacteria from one food to another.
1) Be aware that bacteria from raw meat, soil, eggs and poultry can be easily transferred to surfaces, equipment and hands, which in turn can 'pass on' the bacteria to other foods.
2) Use separate knives and chopping boards for preparing raw meat.
3) Wash your hands after handling raw meat.
4) Never sit raw meat and cooked meat together. Don't allow the blood and juices of raw foods to drip onto cooked foods, e.g. during storage in refrigerators.

There are Other Important Rules for Keeping Food Safe

As well as avoiding cross-contamination:
1) Thaw foods fully before cooking — especially poultry (see p14), which has a high risk of carrying salmonella bacteria.
2) Cook foods thoroughly, especially high-risk foods, which should reach a temperature of above 72°C in the centre of the food. (You could use a digital thermometer to check this.)
3) Even when keeping foods warm they should still be in the region of 70°C — but try not to keep food warm for longer than an hour.
4) Reheat foods to the correct temperature (at least 72°C) for at least three minutes.
5) If food is to be served cold or stored, cool it down as quickly as possible.
6) Keep food covered (away from flies) and in the refrigerator if possible.

I reckon shark steak's a fairly high-risk food myself...

Not only will learning this stuff help you through your GCSE, it'll save your stomach lots of grief. Top marks and top health or dodgy marks and worse guts — the choice is yours.

Section Three — Food Processes

Industrial Equipment

The food industry makes big piles of food. And big piles of food calls for big, computerised equipment. These CAM machines *(see p23)* are the big Daddies of the cooking-tool world...

Computerised Scales are the Best

Accurate weighing is essential for consistency and quality. Digital scales are more effective and accurate than balance scales. Computerised scales are even better. They:

1) Weigh accurately to within 0.05 g.
2) Can be preset to weigh a variety of ingredients.
3) Can be linked to the main computer so that feedback is immediate (e.g. no more ingredients are added when a certain weight is reached).
4) Enable products which are underweight or overweight to be rejected.

Depositors are Huge Tubes which Fill Containers

Depositors are huge tubes, nozzles or funnels which fill containers like pastry cases and moulds.

1) They are usually linked to a computer for control.
2) The filling can be aerated (mousse-like) semi-solid, viscous or liquid.
3) A measured amount is deposited each time.
4) A variety of shapes and sizes of nozzles or ends may be used.

Industry uses Large-Scale Ovens

Industrial ovens are usually computer-controlled and come in all shapes and sizes:

1) Tunnel oven: the products (e.g. biscuits) travel on a conveyor belt through an oven which is lit by a series of burners or heated elements.
2) Deck oven: for batches of products (e.g. bread) to be cooked at the same time. Often the dry heat works in conjunction with steam to give a moist texture to the product.
3) Convection oven: surrounds the products with heat.
4) Travel oven: similar to a tunnel oven but on a larger scale.

And there's Loads of other Equipment as well...

1) Mandolin: used to slice and cut foods evenly every time (and to play Greek folk music).
2) Centrifuge: works like a huge spin dryer and can separate liquid from solid parts.
3) Floor-standing mixers: large food processors which can mix huge quantities of ingredients evenly and consistently every time.
4) Vat: huge container used for cooking foods.
5) Hopper: huge holding container which often has a weighing facility attached to it. It will feed in the correct amount of ingredients, then a valve will shut off the feed system.
6) Silo: another huge holding vessel.
7) Tunnel freezer, cooler or blancher: like a tunnel oven but freezes, cools or blanches instead.

Contenders, ready — Depositors, ready...

The food industry is trying to make huge quantities of food consistently, so they use all sorts of high-tech gadgets for cooking, slicing, storing and freezing the food. It stands to reason — you try producing 100 000 exceedingly good cakes in your kitchen at home.

Section Three — Food Processes

Revision Summary for Section Three

That's another eight pages successfully negotiated. Well, almost. All you've got to do now is go over these questions and check you can remember all the stuff. Any doubt lurking, and it's back to the section for you, my friend. Read back over any bits you're not sure of, then come back to the questions and try again. Keep doing this until you can answer all the questions standing on your head. It ain't fun but it's the recipe for success — recipe... food technology... geddit... (oh my sides...)

1) What is an emulsion?
2) When flour is mixed with water, does it become a solution or a suspension?
3) Name an example of a foam.
4) Name a product which requires pectin in its production.
5) Explain what is meant by batch production.
6) What is the difference between batch production and jobbing production?
7) What is 'downtime'?
8) What does 'CAM' stand for, and what's the point of it anyway?
9) Describe the ideal conditions for bacteria to multiply.
10) Give the common symptoms of food poisoning.
11) What is meant by the term 'a high-risk food'?
    a) a food with a high chance of carrying food poisoning   b) a cucumber with a machine gun
12) What is 'cross-contamination'? Describe three things you can do to avoid it.
13) Give two measures that butchers should take to avoid contamination in pre-prepared Scotch eggs.
14) Describe how could you safely reheat cooked rice.
15) What is the basic principle behind most forms of preservation?
16) Name three methods of preservation, and give a brief description of each one.
17) What's the point of smoking? *This is food tech, remember — I'm not trying to start a deep-and-meaningful.*
18) What does HACCP stand for? Why is it important in the food industry?
19) What is a risk assessment?
20) Set up an HACCP flowchart for decorating a cake. If you're on a roll, have a go at making a pizza as well. Well, I mean have a go at setting up an HACCP flowchart for making a pizza.
21) Say one good thing about breadmaking machines.
22) Why might a food manufacturer choose to use a large free-standing electric mixer for the production of large quantities of cake mixture?
23) What health and safety precautions would people need to take when using a freestanding electric mixer?
24) What's the advantage of computerised scales over balance scales?
25) Name two different kinds of large-scale ovens used in industry, and give a brief description of how they work.
26) Which of these is a machine for chopping food?
    a) a lute   b) a bouzouki   c) a mandolin   d) a hurdy gurdy

Section Three — Food Processes

SECTION FOUR — MARKETING AND INDUSTRY

Different Target Groups

Manufacturers don't just produce a product and hope people will buy it.
They look for a group of people with specific needs and design a product to fit those needs.

The Target Group are the Consumers a Product is Made for

1) Manufacturers develop products for different groups of people.
2) It's important to develop the product so that it fits their needs and preferences.

> If you're developing your own product you need to work out what your target group is early on. You should take their preferences and views about what the product should be like into consideration. For example, you could get them to help you trial the product.

Dietary Groups have Specific Nutritional Needs

A target group might have different nutritional and dietary needs, for example:

1) Babies and toddlers need nutrients for growth and development.
2) Pregnant and /or breastfeeding women need extra protein, calcium and iron.
3) Elderly people may need to cut down on fats and carbohydrates.
4) Diabetics need a healthy diet and have to control carbohydrates and sugar.
5) Vegetarians, particularly vegans, may need extra vitamin B12.
6) Athletes and people with active jobs want foods that provide energy.
7) Slimmers and people with inactive jobs need to eat low-fat foods.

Manufacturers also Target Specific Preferences

Not all target groups are defined by nutritional needs — manufacturers also target people's preferences. A product might be designed to appeal to people who want to eat in a hurry or want organic food or like snacking in front of the TV — they're all target groups.

It's okay looking at what people need nutritionally, but a lot of people don't think, "Yes I'll buy that because it is good for me and contains essential nutrients."
People buy products for a variety of the following reasons:

1) They look good.
2) They taste good.
3) They're trendy.
4) The packaging is appealing.
5) They can be cooked quickly.
6) They're environmentally friendly.
7) They're cheap and affordable.
8) They're posh, quality food — and never mind the expense.
9) They're easy to eat — important for very young kids and ill people.

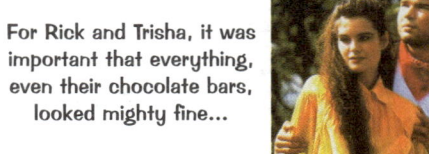

For Rick and Trisha, it was important that everything, even their chocolate bars, looked mighty fine...

chocolate bar bandana

None of that explains who buys all-day-breakfast in a tin...

It's a bit freaky really. You think you're buying something of your own free will, but really there's a manufacturer somewhere going, "Ha — I knew they'd go for those low-fat, organic, pink crisps."

Other Factors Affecting People's Choices

Some people worry about the environmental and health effects of the food they eat. They might choose organic food or stuff with packaging they can recycle.

Environmental Issues Affect the Manufacturing Industry

Most food you buy is packaged — and the waste packaging makes up 70% of household rubbish. Environmentally this is a very bad thing *(no, really?)* because:

1) Packaging of mass-produced products uses large amounts of material.
2) It often gets used once and then thrown away — a waste of the materials and a big contribution to Britain's already huge waste dumps.
3) Some packaging materials, like plastic, take a long time to biodegrade, and could take up space in a waste dump for years.

In 1997 the Government legislated regulations to all businesses which manufacture, fill or sell packaging in excess of 50 tonnes a year. The point was to:

> 1) Increase the amount of packaging which can be recycled.
> 2) Reduce the amount of packaging in total.

Some People Don't Like Genetically Modified Ingredients

Another controversial issue is the production of genetically modified food.

Benefits
1) Crops which can resist disease, insects and viruses so there is less wastage.
2) Plants which can be modified to tolerate herbicides — so weeds die but not the crops. This means a reduction in the use of environmentally unfriendly herbicides.

Concerns
1) The pollen of the genetically modified plants contains the modified gene. This pollen could cross-breed with normal wild plants. As well as interfering with nature, this could result in the creation of 'superweeds'.
2) Consumers also worry because genetically modified food is often not labelled as such and they want to know what they're buying.

Food Additives Make Food Seem More Attractive

Food additives can be added to food to improve its properties — for example:
1) Preserving food by stopping the growth of bacteria and therefore increasing the shelf life. *(See p25.)*
2) Colouring food, especially those products which lose colour during processing, e.g. jam.
3) Keeping food products stable, e.g. emulsifiers, which prevent the separation of liquids.
4) Sweetening a product to make it tastier, e.g. saccharin in drinks.
5) Adding nutritional properties e.g. improving the iron and vitamin content in breakfast cereals.
6) Improving the taste or smell of food products e.g. monosodium glutamate in Chinese food.

There are also disadvantages to food additives:
1) Some people, especially kids, are allergic to certain additives.
2) Some additives, like sweeteners or added salt, make food less healthy.

Some people prefer to buy organic foods which contain no additives or genetically modified ingredients and haven't been grown using pesticides or artificial fertilisers.

Consumers — stop being such fussy whingers...

This page may be boring but at least it's pretty easy... ...that's all there is to say.

Section Four — Marketing and Industry

Standard Food Components

Food manufacturers often use standard food components to make their products...

Standard Food Components are Ready-Made Ingredients

In the food industry manufacturers buy in standard components from other food manufacturers. You will have used standard components in your own cooking:

- stock cubes
- pizza bases
- ready-to-roll icing
- marzipan
- ready-made pastry
- sauces for pasta

Advantages of Using Standard Food Components

1) Saves preparation time. There are fewer stages in the production process, making it quicker.
2) Less effort and skill required by staff.
3) Less machinery and specialist equipment needed — saves money.
4) The quality is guaranteed — the standard food components can be ordered to the right specifications.
5) It ensures consistency of flavour, texture, weight, shape and colour.
6) Can make food preparation safer/more hygienic as high-risk products e.g. chicken, eggs, soiled vegetables can be prepared elsewhere.
7) Components can be bought in bulk.
8) Overall saves the manufacturer money.

TV chef, Ja "wicked" Moliver, used non-standard food components as his gimmick.

Disadvantages of Using Standard Food Components

There are some disadvantages for manufacturers in using standard food components bought from other manufacturers:

- They have to rely on another manufacturer to supply the product. This might be less reliable than doing everything internally.
- The components might be expensive.
- The components might not taste as good as using fresh ingredients.
- Special storage space or conditions might be needed.

Toenails — Non-Standard Food Components...

My boyfriend claims that he bites his toenails. Write in to the usual address if you think this is good grounds for dumping him. And remember to learn everything on this page. Please.

Section Four — Marketing and Industry

Labelling

Labelling on products is important because it gives the consumer information. Customers can use it to make informed decisions and choices about what they buy and eat.

Manufacturers Must Obey the Law

There are several laws which specify what information labels must give. For example:
1) Trade Descriptions Acts (1968)
2) Food Labelling Regulations (1996)
3) Food Safety Act (1990)
4) Food Standards Act (1999)

Food Labels Have to Tell You Certain Information

Legally the label on processed food has to tell you the following information:
1) The name of the product and what it is.
2) What ingredients the product contains, in descending order of weight. Preservatives, colourants, emulsifiers and other additives are listed in the ingredients list.
3) How the product should be stored.
4) The weight or volume of the product.
5) The name and address of the manufacturer.
6) A 'best before' or 'use by' date.
7) Instructions for preparation and cooking.
8) Whether a product contains genetically modified soya or maize ingredients.

Nutritional Information Sometimes has to be Included

- If a special nutritional claim has been made, such as 'low sugar', then products must, by law, show the nutritional information.
- This information is often shown in the form of a table.
- It usually shows energy values and protein, carbohydrate, fat and sodium quantities per 100g or per portion.

NUTRITIONAL INFORMATION	per 100g	per 55g serving
Energy	2180kJ/525 kcal	1199kJ/289 kcal
Protein	6.5g	3.6g
Carbohydrate	50.0g	27.5g
of which sugars	2.0g	1.1g
Fat	33.0g	18.2g
of which saturates	15.0g	8.3g
Sodium	0.7g	0.4g
Fibre	4.0g	2.2g

There are Other Features on Some Labels

A bar code is a series of lines and numbers which enables the product to be electronically identified. Information about the product can be relayed to a computer.

√ Symbols are used to show that food is suitable for a particular diet such as Vegetarian or Gluten Free.

The manufacturer's logo is sometimes included.

Quality Guaranteed or full refund

The manufacturer sometimes includes a guarantee that the product is of high quality.

AAAAAAAAAAAAAAAAAAAAAAAAAarrrrrrrrrrrgggh...

Only one more page to go. It ain't that bad. Just one more little waffer-thin page left — about the scintillating, glamorous, gossip-fest that is... packaging. Hmm.

Section Four — Marketing and Industry

Packaging

Food packaging legislation says that food packaging must not be hazardous to human health, cause food to deteriorate or cause unaccepatable changes in the quality of a product.

Packaging Contains, Protects and Preserves

1) Packaging contains the product neatly.
2) It protects the product from damage during transportation, display and storage. It also protects the product from flies, vermin and people touching the food.
3) Packaging naturally preserves the food and extends its shelf life. Most packaging is sealed so reduces bacterial destruction. Some packaging is part of the preservation process, e.g. tin cans and vacuum packed products.
4) The packaging also identifies and gives customers information about the product.
5) Sometimes the design of the packaging is what attracts the customer to the product.

Different Types of Material are Used for Packaging

1) There are loads of different materials used for packaging — there's one for every occasion:

MATERIAL	ADVANTAGES	DISADVANTAGES
Glass	Strong, transparent, can be recycled, variety of shapes and colours	Heavy, breaks easily
Plastic	Rigid or flexible, lightweight, cheap, variety of colours and shapes, microwavable	Often not recycled, slow to biodegrade
Aluminium	Strong, waterproof, variety of shapes and thicknesses, can be recycled	Expensive
Paper and Board	Colourful, flexible, cheap, can be laminated to make it waterproof, easy to print onto, can be recycled	Not very strong

2) Packaging can be easily produced using CAD/CAM (Computer-Aided Design and Manufacture). CAD software is used to design the packaging, then the information is transferred to a CAM machine, which prints the design then scores and cuts out the packaging.

Changing the Atmosphere Helps Preserve Food

Modified Atmosphere Packaging (MAP) Changes the Proportions of Gases

1) Modified Atmosphere Packaging is used to extend the shelf life of fresh foods.
2) It preserves food in sealed packs containing a mixture of oxygen, nitrogen and carbon dioxide.
3) Foods often packaged in this way include: fresh and cooked meats, fish, fruit and vegetables, fresh pasta and cheese and even bread.
4) However, once the packet has been opened, the food has a normal shelf life.

Vacuum Packaging Keeps Food in Oxygen-Free Conditions

1) Vacuum packing is a way of packaging food that helps to preserve it.
2) All the air is sucked away from around the food and the plastic packaging is sealed.
3) The food is now in anaerobic conditions — no oxygen.
4) Foods commonly sold like this are bacon, fish and coffee.
5) Once the packet is open you have to treat the food according to its normal storage instructions.

All I keep thinking is — "bubble wrap's so cool..."

When you develop a product, try designing the packaging on a computer — include nutritional info, storage instructions and a memorable product name:

David's Golden Meatballs
Food: Stuff to Eat
Small Chickens From Outer Space
Ron's Second Best Soup

Section Four — Marketing and Industry

Revision Summary for Section Four

'The most boring selection of information in the entire history of the world' would not be a fair description of this section. Think about reading the primary school assembly book from cover to cover, or the instructions that come with a vacuum cleaner, or... William Hague's autobiography. There are worse things than Marketing and Industry. So grit your teeth and get it over with — go through these questions as quickly as possible, looking up the bits you don't know. Then go through them once more without looking bits up. Only then will you be free.

1) What is meant by a 'target group'?

2) Name three dietary groups and describe their specific nutritional needs.

3) Name six factors, other than nutrition, that might affect people's choice of food.

4) Explain why excessive packaging is an environmental concern, and describe what the Government did about it in 1997. Write a mini-essay for your answer.

5) Name two advantages and two disadvantages of genetically modified food.

6) Give three reasons for putting additives in food. Then describe two disadvantages of doing this.

7) What is the usual name given to food that has no additives, isn't genetically modified and hasn't been grown using pesticides and artificial fertilisers?

8) What is a standard food component?   a) a ready-made meal   b) a ready-made ingredient
   c) carbohydrate   d) a ready-made orange

9) Give three examples of standard food components that you might use in your own cooking.

10) Give three advantages and three disadvantages, for manufacturers, of using standard food components in their products?

11) Name eight things that legally must be on the label of a food product.

12) Why can packaging be bad for the environment?

13) Name two labelling laws that apply to food manufacturers.

14) List four pieces of information which should be included on a food label.

15) Why is it important to package food products or ingredients?

16) Name a disadvantage of using plastic as a packaging material.

17) Describe Modified Atmosphere Packaging.

18) Does vacuum packaging help to preserve food even after it has been opened?

Section Five — Design and Development

Evaluation & Development

You've seen the design process in Section 1. This section looks at that process **in practice**, so you've got to make sure you've got it in your head.

Remember the *Stages* of Design

1) Work out the **type** of product you intend to develop.
   e.g. cake, fizzy drink, pizza or whatever.

2) Produce a general **specification**. This won't include all the detail of a full design specification (mentioned on page 3), but it will outline the basic idea.

3) Carry out **surveys** and **questionnaires** to find out if there are similar products available to buy in the shops, and if people will buy the type of product being proposed.

> Manufacturers get ideas and then carry out surveys to work out a product which is **different** from the competitor's, but which will **appeal** to the market. They also use **questionnaires** to find out what products people like and to decide the **group of people** they will be aiming their product at (children, teenagers, busy people, the elderly etc).

4) Work out how your product can be **better** than rival products. Then it's full **design specification**, **testing**, **mass production** and dodgy endorsement by Jamie Oliver.

Brainstorm to Produce Initial Ideas

- Brainstorming is a good way to **produce** initial ideas.
- These initial ideas are combined with the results of any surveys carried out, bearing in mind the chosen **target group**.
- It's important to **keep** noting down **WHY** each decision is made. Remember — to say that you have chosen a dish because you "like the taste", **isn't** good enough. WHY do you like the taste? Did the people who helped with your survey like the taste, and if so WHY?
- Brainstorming produces the **FIRST** product idea.
- Once the product idea is decided however, that is only the **beginning** of the development process. That product will be **tested**, **changed**, **compared** and hopefully **improved** until it's just right.

I want to develop a Yorkshire pudding flavoured chewing gum...

Design and development is a long and drawn-out process. You have to get an original idea by thinking about what you want to produce and who it's for. The process of testing, changing and comparing continues until everything is perfect — a bit like revising really.

Evaluation & Development

Once you've got an idea the next stage is to make a PROTOTYPE
— testing prototypes is what design and development is all about.

Try Out Your First Idea

The only way to find out what your food product will be like is to make a version and try it out.

Whilst trying out prototypes, you must write down what you are going to do and why — that way someone else could take your instructions and produce the same product. Include these FIVE things:

1. ingredients used
2. reasons for any choices made
3. equipment used
4. plan of action (instructions for making)
5. selection of tasting and evaluation sheets ready to complete

Tasting and appearance tests are carried out on the product at all stages.
Then adjustments may be made to the recipe to produce a better result.

The tests for tasting and appearance give
information on these aspects of the product:

- The overall appearance
- Texture
- Taste
- Smell

D'ya see what I mean about the slight side effect...

Then Try Another Idea and Compare

The tests on the first prototype might create ideas about what else to try.
Maybe it tasted great but was really expensive — so you could try using some cheaper ingredients.

1. REMEMBER to note down what you are changing and why.
2. Each time a prototype is produced it goes through the same tasting and other tests so that the best product can be selected.
3. Then you can go back and compare the different prototypes and come up with the best product.

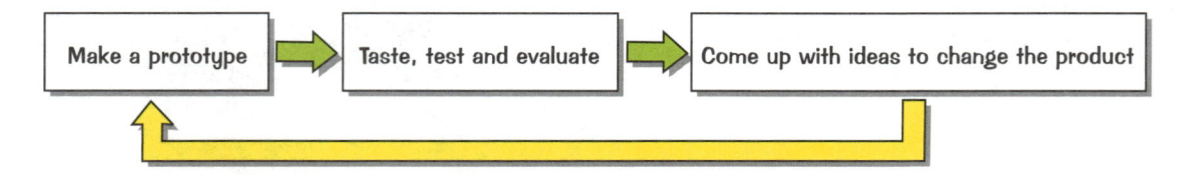

Make a prototype → Taste, test and evaluate → Come up with ideas to change the product

Dehydrated water — it's got to be a winner...

Taste, test, evaluate, change...
                Taste, test, evaluate, change...
                                Taste, test, evaluate, change...

Section Five — Design and Development

Data Collection and Analysis

You can get useful marketing information from a load of different sources and in a variety of ways.

To Develop a New Product you need Information

You need to know:

1. As much info as you can get on similar products already on the market.
2. The likes and dislikes of your potential customers.
3. Costs of producing / selling similar products.
4. Nutritional content — the suitability of products for different dietary requirements.
5. Storage needs — how products should be stored and how long they can be stored for.

You can get this information from:

Magazines and Newspapers:	Can provide information on products on the market, public likes and dislikes and nutritional contents of some foods along with info on different dietary requirements.
Questionnaires:	The likes and dislikes of buyers and the prices people would pay for the product.
Surveys:	Current trends in food, what is already available, costs, buying habits.
Interviews with professional people:	Doctors, dieticians, nurses and shopkeepers are all useful sources of the information you need.
Internet:	It contains loads of information but there's a lot of junk too, so you'll have to be careful that you select only the relevant bits.
Manufacturers:	They are normally happy to send you information.
Disassembly of existing products:	Getting info about structure and content by taking apart similar rival products. (More about this on page 42.)

Then you can Decide what Changes to Make

The information you collect will put you in a better position to consider good product development. The whole point is to come up with an idea of what you can do better with your product. You might identify from your research the need to experiment with things like:

- Changing ingredients — e.g. using healthier options.
- Changing shapes / colours — e.g. if all cola is brown, making yours clear could give it the edge.
- Changing finishes / textures — e.g. using pieces of tomato instead of tomato flavoured sauce.
- Changing packaging — e.g. you might want to appeal to a specific group, such as vegans.
- Adjusting costs — e.g. you could make it more expensive to make it seem more exclusive.

The information you have collected and analysed will help you decide which of your original ideas is the best to develop. You will also get some ideas about how you're going to make your product different from those already out there.

I've got it — chocolate packaging and a cardboard cake...

Can you believe all this effort goes into every chocolate bar and custard tart? Mind you, if they put all this effort into improving food ideas, then why does somebody still make pickled haddock with curry and pineapple sauce... It's true — they do, I just heard it on the radio. Urghh.

Section Five — Design and Development

Questionnaires

Questionnaires are a simple way of doing market research to find out the views
and preferences of your possible customers or target group.

There's a Standard Way of Writing Questionnaires

When you write a questionnaire you should include:

1) A title — for example it could be 'Questionnaire Researching Favourite Puddings'.
2) A brief explanation of the purpose of the questionnaire.
3) A mixture of questions, so the person filling it in doesn't get bored.

There are three basic types of questions:

1) Closed Questions — require simple YES/NO answers, e.g. do you like puddings?
   A questionnaire with this type of question saves loads of time.
   Analysing is easy and you can then show clear results at the end.

2) Open Questions — have no set answer, e.g. what's your favourite pudding?
   They allow people an opportunity to provide details and give their opinion.

   This type of questioning is very time-consuming and requires extra time to draw conclusions
   from the results. You could, however, gain a great deal of valuable information.

3) Multiple choice questions — give a choice of answers,
   e.g. What puddings do you prefer?
   Chocolate type puddings ☐   Ice cream type puddings ☐   Slug type puddings ☐

Think Carefully About What You Want to Find Out

It's important that you think through what information you need before you write your questions.
You'll probably want to find out the following:

1) Some information about the person answering your questions.
   - Are they male or female?
   - What age bracket are they in? (11-15, 16-20, 21-25 etc)
2) Do they already buy the kind of product you're thinking of developing?
3) What do they want from that type of product?
   Do they like a particular flavour or colour?
4) When and where do they buy it and where do they consume it?
   E.g. They might buy it at a local newsagent and eat it on the bus to school.
5) Will they want to buy your version of the product?
   Explain the advantage of your product over existing brands
   — would that be enough to tempt them to buy your version?
6) Is there something they would like from that product that existing brands don't have?

To eat or not to eat? — That is the question...

Don't choose cheesecake as the subject of your questionnaire. You'll just make yourself hungry.
Just writing this page I was starting to drool and yell, "Please. Someone. Get me to the bakery."

Section Five — Design and Development

Presenting and Analysing Results

Results need to be presented so that they're <u>useful</u> for the product development and can be easily <u>interpreted</u> by others. It's the same in industry and for you when you're doing your coursework.

You Can Show Results in Lots of Different Ways

A questionnaire needs to be answered by a <u>variety</u> of people. It depends on the scale of the project — but a <u>big chocolate company</u> might ask <u>hundreds</u> of people. (For your coursework try and get at least <u>20 responses</u>.)

The <u>information</u> from a pile of questionnaires is much easier to understand if it's put into <u>tables</u> and <u>graphs</u>.

Using the right type of chart or graph can make a big difference to how easy the information is to understand:

> **PIE CHARTS:** are great for showing percentages or proportions.
>
> **LINE GRAPHS:** are useful for showing trends.
>   E.g. Are people eating more cream cakes over recent months or years?
>
> **BAR CHARTS:** are useful for the 'How often' type of questions.
>
> <u>3D charts</u> can make information look great, but get it wrong and it'll look <u>confusing</u>. It's better to keep it simple and clear.

Favourite cheesecake flavour

50 people aged 16 - 60 were asked their favourite cheesecake flavour, given the options listed in the chart.

You can produce all these graphs and charts by <u>hand</u> drawing — but if you can use a <u>computer</u> you'll gain extra marks for the use of ICT.

Graphs and Charts are Useless if they're not Labelled

OK, so you've probably heard this before, but every graph or chart must have:

- A TITLE
- LABELS ON EACH AXIS
- LABELS OR DESCRIPTIONS ON EACH SECTION OF THE PIE CHART

Analyse the Results — What Kind of Product Would Sell?

1) Look carefully at the <u>information</u> you've got and make some <u>conclusions</u> about the <u>market</u> there is for your product, and what you need to <u>do next</u> to <u>develop</u> your product.
2) Use the results of your questionnaire to <u>answer basic questions</u>: do people like this kind of food? How much are they prepared to pay? Would they be prepared to try a new brand?

It's 'Steak and Kidney' in at number 1, pop pickers...

This all happens in industry — they collect the information, present it in charts and graphs and use that to develop ideas for the products they will make. That advice could come in handy when you're doing your food technology coursework as well — nudge, nudge, wink, wink...

Section Five — Design and Development

Product Analysis

Manufacturers rarely develop a totally brand new product — they usually redesign an existing one. Before they start, they do a product analysis on an existing product to find ways of improving it.

Start with Disassembly and Package Analysis

Disassembly means taking a product apart and examining the bits. Food technologists in industry always analyse similar products and you'll have to do the same for your coursework — so listen up.

> Draw the package and the food. Then add notes and labels about the following:
>
> 1. The measurements and weights of the product. Make a table of ingredients with the weight of each written in. For example if you are disassembling a cheese and tomato sandwich, weigh the cheese, tomato and bread for your table. This will give you the proportions of each thing.
> 2. Note down the textures and colours of the various ingredients.
> 3. Examine how the product is put together and make notes about how you think it was made.

Use the packaging to find out more detail about the product.

- List the ingredients (with weights) you haven't covered by disassembly.
- The style and text give clues about the target market, e.g. using cartoons to target young kids.
- The nutritional value of the product shows you how healthy it is.
- Cooking and storage instructions give you information about the life and use of the product.
- Make a note of how expensive it is.

Now add notes about how it looks, tastes and smells.
Make sure your notes are specific and to the point. For example:

✓ "It looks dry, with very little shine"   ✗ "It doesn't look very nice"

Use the Info to Make Your Product Better than Theirs

After you've analysed a product, look at its faults and write down ways you could improve upon them to make your product better. *(See also p39.)* Possible improvements include:

1. The quality and quantity of the ingredients.
2. The size, shape and weight of the finished product.
3. Appearance, texture and flavour.
4. The quality and effectiveness of the packaging and the text on the packaging.
5. The price — if it's too expensive for what it is, say why, and by how much.

When you're writing out your suggested improvements, be precise.
Don't use 'woolly' words or phrases like "It looks ugly, so we should make it look nicer".

Get me a drill — prepare to be disassembled, Mr Scone...

There's no point in reinventing the wheel, so food producers look at other products on the market and think about how they can change or improve them to make their product marketable.

Section Five — Design and Development

Sensory Analysis

Sensory analysis testing — the manufacturers do it and so can you.

Sensory Analysis is a Way of Finding Out What People Like

Sensory analysis is giving people samples of food and asking their opinion about its appearance, taste, smell and texture (using their senses). It gives manufacturers an idea of what consumers think about a food product. Manufacturers use sensory testing:

1) when a new product is being developed — to see whether people like it
2) on existing products — to find out ways of improving them
3) on competitors' products — to find out what's good about them

Sensory Analysis can be done in different ways and using various tests. For example:

1) Ranking or Rating Testing

In this type of test people are asked to rank a number of similar products:

Ranking Test	Name: Delia Quiff
Taste the samples and place them in order of preference	
Sample code	Order of Preference
SPE12	2
SPE14	1

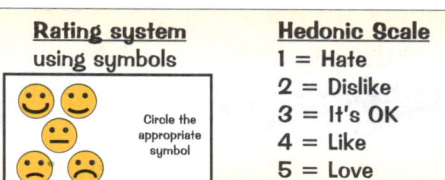

Rating system using symbols — Circle the appropriate symbol

Hedonic Scale
1 = Hate
2 = Dislike
3 = It's OK
4 = Like
5 = Love

2) Star Diagrams

The main characteristics of a product are chosen and testers are asked to rate them on a rating scale of 1-5. Each leg of the star diagram represents a characteristic, and the ratings score for it is marked on it. The marks can then be joined up (looking a bit like a star). The diagram shows visually which characteristics are popular and which aren't.

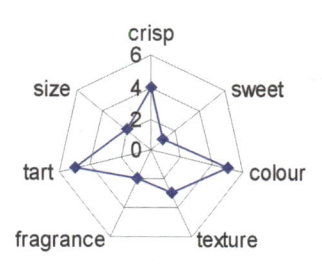

3) Triangle Testing

- This is when testers are given three samples and asked to say which is the 'odd one out'.
- Manufacturers use it if they are trying to develop a cheap or low-fat version of a food that tastes the same as the original. The testers would be given two samples of the original and one of the new version.

Use Sensory Analysis Testing for Your Product

Once you have made your product you need a group of people to be testers for the sensory analysis. It could be your family or a group of friends or, better still a small group of people who fit your target group.

1) Set up a quiet area where people will not be disturbed or influenced by other people.
2) Supply cups of water to sip between samples to refresh the palate.
3) Use small quantities of food with clean utensils. Don't allow people to put used spoons in your food.
4) Use codes or symbols for the products, to prevent the tasters being influenced by the name.
5) Make sure the tasters understand your ranking system.

Analyse This... small piece of raw potato...

Section Five — Design and Development

Control Systems and Feedback

Systems are sets of separate things which work together to result in a task being completed. When systems are used they are often broken down into manageable units.

Systems are Used for All Sorts...

Systems are used for things like:
- Making the process you're going to use more efficient
- To make the task you are carrying out easier
- Making the task and process easier to check

A system is usually divided into three parts:

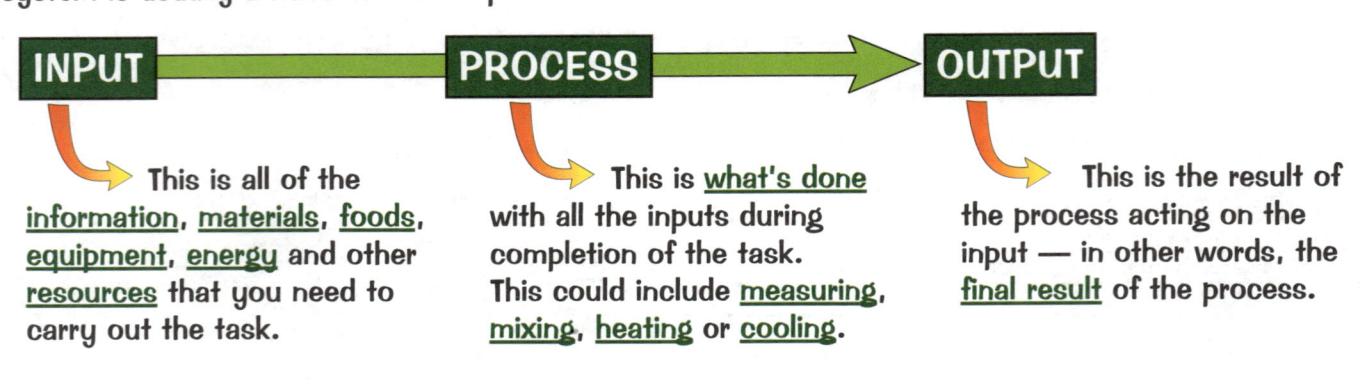

INPUT → **PROCESS** → **OUTPUT**

- **INPUT:** This is all of the information, materials, foods, equipment, energy and other resources that you need to carry out the task.
- **PROCESS:** This is what's done with all the inputs during completion of the task. This could include measuring, mixing, heating or cooling.
- **OUTPUT:** This is the result of the process acting on the input — in other words, the final result of the process.

Systems Include Processes which give Feedback

Feedback may be used at each stage of production and helps to ensure good quality final products.

For example, if a pizza is being completely covered with cheese, this can be checked by a person or perhaps by a machine. If the pizza is completely covered then it can be cooked. If not, the pizza has to go back to the beginning of that stage of the process.

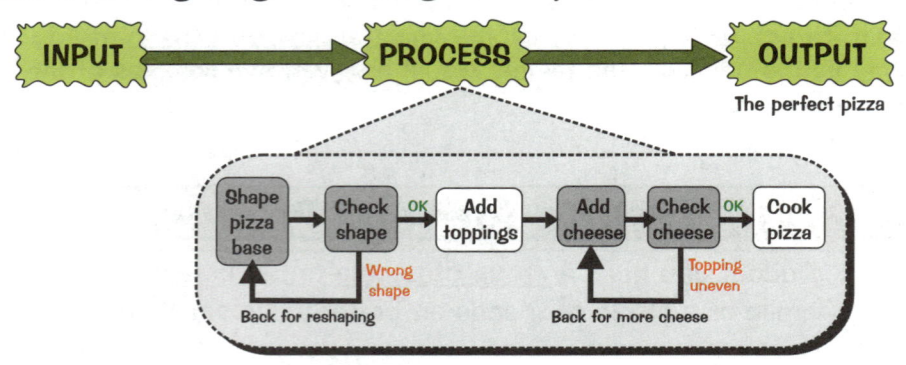

INPUT → **PROCESS** → **OUTPUT** (The perfect pizza)

Process detail: Shape pizza base → Check shape (OK) → Add toppings → Add cheese → Check cheese (OK) → Cook pizza. Wrong shape: Back for reshaping. Topping uneven: Back for more cheese.

A computer may monitor a manufacturing process at each stage and give feedback. It may then take control and return the product to a previous process stage.

This would be an example of COMPUTER-AIDED MANUFACTURE (CAM) — also see page 28-29.

System addict — I never can give it up*...

You put a load if stuff in (INPUT), you do something to it (PROCESS) and you get something out in the end (OUTPUT) — that's a SYSTEM. In addition you can add feedback which checks the product is OK and allows problems to be fixed. Cool eh...

Section Five — Design and Development

This is for your teacher — get them to read it out and see if they start singing and shaking their 1980s booty.

Quality Control and Assurance

Manufacturers want customer loyalty — so they need to make sure their product is always manufactured to a high standard. These are the industry jargon words for it:

QUALITY ASSURANCE (QA) is all about standards — setting standards and meeting them.
QUALITY CONTROL (QC) is how you check whether you're meeting those standards. *(See below.)*

Manufacturers have a System to Deal with Faults

To ensure that a food product leaves the factory in good condition the manufacturer has to set up a foolproof system of checking and dealing with faults.

- Throughout the manufacturing process, food products are visually checked and tested.
- Products can be checked against the detailed manufacturer's specification.
- Part of the system is feedback. If a product is not right, the information is immediately relayed back to the factory floor so the problem can be fixed quickly.

Mass-Produced Products Need to be of Identical Quality

1) To ensure accurate weight the ingredients are weighed on electronic scales. The final product is also weighed — and taken off the production line if it is overweight or underweight.
2) To ensure accurate size or shape, standardised moulds, templates and cutting devices are used.
3) The same flavour and texture is produced every time by using standard food components and accurately measured ingredients. Preparation, mixing and cooking times are also fixed.
4) The same colour is produced by using fixed ingredients, cooking times and temperatures. Sometimes the colour of the product is checked by a machine against the standard colour.
5) The way the product is packaged is also controlled.
6) The manufacturer may print details on the packaging, saying who the consumer should contact if the product is substandard.

Hazard Analysis Critical Control Points (HACCP)

HACCP is a system which reduces the risk of food being damaged or contaminated before it reaches the consumer. All possible hazards are identified and controls are put in place. There's lots more info about HACCP on pages 26 and 27.

Finally the Product is Tested by Quality Control

- Quality control usually takes place at the end of a process and involves inspection, sampling and testing.
- There is usually a Quality Control Department within the factory, which takes charge of all the testing and inspections.
- It will also insist on putting in place whatever controls are necessary to ensure a quality product. The whole workforce will be involved in this system of controlling and checking.

"Hard cheese..." *(I love Terry Thomas. What a man. One day, when you're very old and a bit bored, watch 'School for Scoundrels'.)*

Old age has advantages. You can get up in the morning, have a good yell at a stressed editor trying to get to work, then go back to bed with a nice cuppa. But the bitterness of the editor never dies.*

*Note to old people — don't shout at editors. We have the power of the written word and the occasional empty tip box in which to wreak our vengeance.

Revision Summary for Section Five

No two ways about it — there's a load of stuff to learn in this section. Nine pages full of questionnaires, tests, analysis, systems and quality control. It's enough to give you a brainstorm of your own. But it's no good crying over spilt milk — there it is and it's got to be learnt. "How?" I hear you cry. Simply answer these questions, check any bits you don't know and then answer these questions again. Keep going until you've got it all sussed. Sound familiar? This is the way of CGP, this is the way it has always been...

1) Why do manufacturers carry out surveys?
2) Explain what a brainstorm is and why it's an important process.
3) What is a prototype?
4) Why do manufacturers carry out evaluations?
5) Why is it important for detailed instructions to be available for a manufacturer or you?
6) Why do manufacturers carry out tastings and tests on products under development?
7) a) List four pieces of information that a manufacturer would need in order to make decisions on new products.
   b) For each answer to a), list a couple of possible sources of that kind of information.
8) Having investigated the products on the market, list four things a manufacturer may wish to change or improve on, when creating a new food for sale.
9) Describe three different types of question that could be used during research.
10) Give four examples of questions you could ask. (Vary the types of question used.)
11) Why is it important to present data clearly in chart form?
12) If you draw a chart that's not labelled, is it:
    a) useless, b) pointless, c) completely pointless, or d) all of the above?
13) What is meant by 'disassembly of a food product'?
15) Name at least five things that are looked for when carrying out a disassembly.
16) List four types of sensory evaluation.
17) Describe how you would set up a sensory analysis so that it would be accurate and fair.
18) Why are systems used?
19) Name the three main parts of any system.
20) What is feedback used for?
21) What does CAM mean?
22) Give an example of how computers can help with manufacture.
23) What is meant by 'quality control' and 'quality assurance'?
24) Describe how manufacturers check that all their food products leave the factory without faults. Name six food qualities that are checked in this process.

Section Five — Design and Development

SECTION SIX — PROJECT ADVICE

Tips on Getting Started

This section's got all the stuff people don't do that the examiners get really annoyed about. Read this before you start your project to make sure you keep those markers happy.

Step 1 — Get your Idea

You can get ideas from different places — for example, your teacher might:
1) tell you exactly what your task is.
2) give you a range of different tasks to choose from.
3) leave the project choice completely up to you.

Don't choose anything Too Easy or Too Boring

Choose a project that will:
1) stretch you and let you demonstrate just how good you are. If the project's too easy, or contains little scope for design, then you'll lose valuable marks.
2) be interesting and challenging enough to keep you motivated. Coursework's a long old process, and you need to stay committed.
3) give you the opportunity to produce a wide range of research, and demonstrate your ICT skills.
4) allow for a variety of solutions, resulting in one which can be completed before the deadline (and this includes allowing time for testing and evaluation to take place).

The Design Brief — Give Loads of Detail

See page 1 for more on the design brief.

1) Your idea needs to have "real commercial potential".
2) You need to describe exactly what you're trying to do.
3) Explain all the factors you need to consider — things like price, weight, market trends, etc.

Say Why your Research is Relevant

1) DON'T just plonk bits of paper in your research folder without any explanation.
2) DON'T just copy and paste stuff from the net either.
3) DO write notes on every piece of research to say why it's relevant, how it changed your thinking or how it backed up your existing ideas.
4) DO refer back to the research section throughout the project — that shows the markers that you've used your research.

See page 2 for more on research.

THIS IS ALL YOU NEED TO DO:

Print or photocopy the relevant stuff. → This is my groovy research that I got off the Internet. This is my groovy research that I got off the Internet. This is my groovy research that I got off the Internet.

Highlight the really useful bits. → *This is my groovy research that I got off the Internet. This is my groovy research that I got off the Internet.* This is my groovy research that I got off the Internet. This is my groovy research that I got off the Internet. This is my groovy research that I got off the Internet.

Write brief notes saying where you found it... → *I found this on Bob's Groovy Tennis Ball Website (www.bobsballs.co.uk).*

...what you found out... → *The highlighted part explains how the fluorescent yellow fur affects the aerodynamics of the ball.*

...and what effect it's had on your project. → *I hadn't previously considered the effect this could have, so I will now factor the use of different materials into my testing.*

Remember — your research analysis will contain all the conclusions from research. But these notes will help you write that research analysis, and will also help the examiner understand why you made your decisions.

Tips on Development

If you're smart you'll keep planning and evaluating throughout your project. If you're a buffoon you'll do a bit at the start, then forget about it and get a bad mark for your project.

You Need a Wide Range of Ideas — Be Creative

1) There's more than one way to skin a cat.
2) Consider plenty of different ways to solve the problem.
3) Don't just come up with one good idea and stick with it. You'll only be sure it's the best idea if you've thought about other ways of doing it.
4) The examiners do really get annoyed about this one — so get those creative juices flowing.

Developing your Ideas — Try Out a Few Alternatives

1) The same goes for developing ideas as for creating them.
2) There's still more than one way to skin a cat.
3) Once you've got the idea, there are still plenty of ways to turn that into an ace product.

Do Loads of Planning — and Not Just at the Start

Planning is for life, not just for... um... the start of your project.
These are the things you should do:

OVERALL PROJECT PLAN AT THE START:

1) to help you focus on the task
2) to make sure you know what stage you should have reached at various times — this way, if you fall behind schedule, you'll know about it as soon as possible, and can do something about it
3) to allow enough time for all the different stages of the design process — including testing, evaluation, and writing up your project

Remember to include testing and evaluating in your time plan — it's all too easy to forget them...

PLAN YOUR RESEARCH:

Work out what research you need to do, and how long you're going to allow yourself for each bit (e.g. questionnaires, disassembling a competing product, and so on).

DON'T GET BOGGED DOWN:

When you're generating proposals or developing your product, don't spend too long working on one little aspect of the product. There's a lot to do — so try to keep your project moving forward.

I have a cunning plan...

OK, repeat after me: "I will allow time for testing in my time plan. I will allow time for testing in my time plan. I will allow time for testing in my time plan. I will allow time for testing in my time plan..."

Tips on Evaluation

Evaluation means examining and judging your work (and you have to do this as part of your project — it's not just something for the examiner to do). If your product doesn't work, but you explain why, you can still get good marks.

Test and Evaluate your Product Throughout the Project

I quote:

> "To be achieving the highest marks in this section, candidates must show that they have used a clear and objective testing strategy."

That's from one of the Chief Examiners' Reports.
(In other words, it's important.)

Don't Wait until you're Finished to Evaluate your Work

1) Like any designer, it's a good idea to be thinking about evaluation from the moment you start working on your design brief.

2) Make notes on your designs and developments as you go along, explaining what was good and bad about each one.

3) When you're writing up your final evaluation, you can also think about whether you'd do anything differently if you were starting again. It's okay if you made some bad decisions during your project — everyone does. But you can get marks if you explain why they were bad decisions, and what you wish you'd done instead.

Check your Brief and Specification

You need to evaluate your product fully. Use these guidelines:

1) Compare your final product to your brief and specification. Does your product satisfy all the conditions it's supposed to? If not, why not?

2) Try to get a likely user (or an expert in this kind of product, maybe) to trial your product and give their honest opinions. This will give you a realistic view of whether it's fit for its purpose — e.g. does it do what it is meant to? And if it does, how well? They may also be able to give you ideas for possible improvements.

3) It's dead important to think about possible improvements you could make as well, such as...

> 1) Time implications — did you spend too much time in one area, or rush to finish?
> 2) Practical work — were you completely satisfied with the quality of your final product?
> 3) Would you approach aspects of your design and development work in a different way?

Never forget to check your briefs...

Everyone makes mistakes (well, everyone except me, obviously). More specifically, everyone makes mistakes in their D and T projects. So don't worry too much when it happens to you. Just explain what went wrong and how you'd avoid it in the future. You can get marks for that.

Section Six — Project Advice

Presentation

It's no use doing a stonking project if your presentation's naff. You've put a lot of time and effort into your project (probably) so it would be a shame for you to mess it up at the last stage.

IT REALLY IS WORTH PUTTING IN THOSE FEW EXTRA HOURS.

The Finished Product — Good Photographs are Ace

Your evaluation should be clearly presented and easy to read.

1) Include an introduction to give a bit of background information — e.g. how you came to think of this project.

2) Always take photos of any non-permanent work — either with a normal or a digital camera. You can manually glue in the print or place the digital image into a word-processed document — whatever suits.

If you're doing *food technology*, photographs are an absolute **MUST**.

It's the only way of getting a lasting record of your work — and the examiners **REALLY WANT** you to do it.

3) Use a mixture of media to present your project. Sure, it's good to show off how nifty you are with CAD or that desktop publishing program. Just don't forget about old-fashioned words to explain what you did, and sketches and prototypes to show how you did it.

4) Split up your evaluation into different sections to make it easy to read. Give each section a clear heading.

The sections could include:
a) how well your product satisfies the brief and specification
b) results from user trials
c) problems you encountered
d) improvements for the future

5) Think about how it fits together — your project needs to work as a whole. It should flow seamlessly from one bit to the next — don't just shove loads of separate bits in with no clue as to how they fit together.

Vocabulary — use the Right Technical Terms

BIG, FANCY WORDS:

1) Do yourself a favour — learn all the technical terms relevant to your subject.
2) And how to spell them.
3) And don't worry if you sound poncy.
4) Using the right technical terms impresses the examiners. They say so in their reports.

GRAMMAR, SPELLING, PUNCTUATION:

1) Treat your project like an English essay.
2) Get your spellings right. Double-check any words you often get wrong.
3) Remember to use full stops and capital letters and write in proper sentences.
4) Short sentences make your work clearer. Long sentences, with loads of commas, can often get very confusing, because it's easy, once you get to the end of the sentence, to forget what you were reading right at the start.
5) Structure your work in paragraphs — a new paragraph for a new topic.

Santa cheats at presentation — he uses elves...

Make sure you stick roughly within your area. If you're doing food technology there's no sense in building a wooden pizza. It should be made with food — flour, tomato, mozzarella, garlic... mmm...

Section Six — Project Advice

Digital Camera

I've said it once and I'll say it again, in food tech you've got to use photos — and if you can get your hands on a digital camera then all the better...

A Digital Camera can Show Off your Work

When you've made a product, take a picture of it as evidence of your 'making'.
They often look better in the photograph.

1) Arrange the finished product attractively (use garnish, an attractive dish or get its best side).
2) Use the 'crop' facility to get rid of any excess area.
3) Don't print the photograph huge just to take up some space. They'll notice.
4) Use the photographs in a variety of ways to enhance and show off what you've made.

Use Photos In the Manufacturer's Specification

In industry, photos of the finished product are included in the manufacturer's specification.
That way the manufacturers will know exactly what the finished dish should look like.
To look really good you could do the same in your manufacturer's specification.

Use Photos in a Flow Chart

Food products can be photographed at different stages and incorporated into a flow chart to show the stages in making.

Making the Perfect Pizza

Add the puree to the pizza base → Sprinkle on grated cheese → Add toppings → Put in the oven → Remove from the oven and slice → Munch away

Use Photos to show Modifications and Improvements

In experimental work (which counts towards your 'making' grade), you can use photographs to show the changes which occurred when recipes were modified.

Use Photos On the Packaging

A good way of showing off your IT skills (which you are graded on) is to design the packaging.
If you use digital pictures of your product on the packaging it can look very professional.

OK, can I go home now?...

In food technology it's not just your food skills that are being tested. You're graded on your IT skills as well. Knowing about digital cameras and using them to your advantage can really boost your coursework mark — so get snapping. Digital imaging software might help too. Right, I'm off.

Section Six — Project Advice

Summary Checklist

This stuff can really make your project *sparkle*.
That's why I've given it a whole extra page — so you can't forget any of it.
Before you hand in your project, make sure you've covered all of these bits,
and you'll be well on your way to DT heaven. ☺

Sparkly Project Checklist

☐ 1) My design brief has got loads of detail.

☐ 2) I've done plenty of research, and said why it's relevant.

☐ 3) I've made a detailed design specification.

☐ 4) I've come up with a wide range of project proposals.

☐ 5) I've included different ways of developing my product, and explained why I made my decisions.

☐ 6) I've tested my product on consumers.

7) I've done loads of planning, including:

  ☐ a) a production plan (time plan),

  ☐ b) planning for mass production.

☐ 8) I've evaluated my product throughout the project.

☐ 9) I've taken photos of everything that won't last.

☐ 10) I've used a mixture of media to present my project.

☐ 11) I've checked my spelling and grammar.

☐ 12) I've used the right technical terms.

Section Six — Project Advice

Index

A
additives 32
aeration 20
aesthetics 4
anaemia 16
analysing results 41
analysis 39
ascorbic acid 16
assurance 45

B
bacteria 24, 25
baked rat 45
bar charts 41
bar code 34
batch production 23
bogged down 49
bottling 25
biological hazards 26, 27
brainstorm 4, 37
bran 13
breadmaker 28
buffoon 48
bulbs 17
bulking agent 11
butter 19

C
CAD 35, 51
calciferol 16
calcium 16
CAM 23, 28, 29, 35, 44
canning 25
carbohydrates 10 - 13
carotene 16
centrifuge 29
cereals 12
checklist 53
cheese 19
chemical hazards 26, 27
cholesterol 18
closed questions 40
coagulate 20
commercial potential 47
computerised scales 29
contamination 24
continuous production 23
control point 26, 27
control systems 44
cream 19
crop 52
cross-contamination 24
cross sections 4

D
dairy products 19
data collection 39
dehydrated water 38
depositors 29
design 1, 37
design brief 1, 47
design process 1
design specification 3
development 5, 38
domestic equipment 28
diabetics 31
dietary groups 31
digital camera 50, 51
disaccharide 10
disassembling 2, 42
drawing techniques 4
drying 25
duck-filled-fatty-puss 15

E
eggs 20
electrical equipment 28
electric whisk 28
elves 50
emulsification 20
emulsion 22
endosperm 13
environmental issues 32
equipment 28
evaluation 6, 38, 49

F
fats 18
faults 45
feedback 29, 44
fibre 16
fish 15
flour 12, 13
flow chart 51
foam 22
folic acid 16
Food Labelling Regulations 34
food poisoning 24
food processor 28
Food Safety Act 34
Food Standards Act 34
formative evaluation 6
freezing 25
fruit 16, 17

G
Gantt chart 8
garnish 17
genetically modified 32, 34
gelatinisation 11
gel 22
gelling 11
gluten 12
grammar 49
guppie (don't eat me) 54

H
HACCP 26, 27, 45
hazard 26, 27
high biological value (HBV) 14
high risk foods 24
homogenisation 19
hopper 29
hygiene 28

I
ICT 41
idea 47
industrial equipment 29
ingredients 22
initial design specification 3
input 44
internet 47
iron 16
irradiation 25
isometric projection 4

J
jamming 25
jobbing production 23

K
killer 12

L
labelling 34
lecithin 20, 22
Leonard Cohen 11
line graph 41
low biological value (LBV) 14

M
maize 12
mandolin 29
manufacturer's specification 7
MAP 25, 35
marinating 15
market research 6
mass production 45
measuring 2
meat 14
meat replacements 15
media 50
meringue 22
microwave 28
milk 19
milling 13
minerals 16
modelling 5
modification 5
modified starch 11
monosaccharide 10
mood board 4
multiple choice questions 40

N
niacin 16
NSP 10, 16, 17
nutritional needs 31
nutritional information 31, 34

O
oils 18
open questions 40
organic 31, 32

Index

orthographic projection 4
osteoporosis 16
output 44
ovens 29

P
package analysis 42
packaging 35
pasteurisation 19, 25
pectin 22
perfect pizza 51
photographs 50
physical hazards 26, 27
pickles 25
pie chart 41
planning production 8
poultry 14
preferences 31
presentation 50
presenting results 41
preservation 25
process 44
product analysis 42
production 23
production process 7
project plan 48
proposals 4
protein 14, 15
prototype 23, 38
punctuation 50

Q
quality assurance (QA) 45
quality control (QC) 45
questionnaires 2, 40
quorn 15

R
ranking test 43
rating test 43
ready made ingredients 33
research 6, 48

retinol 16
riboflavin 16
risk 26, 27
risk assessment 26
rubbish 32 (amongst other pages)

S
safety 28
Sale of Goods Act 34
salmonella 14, 20
salting 25
sampling 45
saturated fats 18
sensory analysis 43
soft flour 12
specification 3, 37
sketches 5
silo 29
smart starches 11
smoking 25
solution 22
soya 15
spelling 51
spreadsheets 7
spina bifida 16
standard food components 33
starch 10, 11
star diagram 43
strong flour 12
sugar 10
summative evaluation 8
superweeds 32
suspension 11, 22
syneresis 11

T
tables 41
target groups 31, 40
technical terms 50
testing 6, 45
textures 42
thiamin 16
thickening agent 11, 20

time plan 48
tin cans 35
tofu 15
tolerances 7
tuber 17
Trade Descriptions Acts 34
triangle testing 43
TVP 15

U
UHT 19
unsaturated fats 18

V
vacuum packed 35
vat 29
vegetables 16, 17
vegetarians 31
vinegar 25
vocabulary 51
vitamins 16

W
weights 42
Wham 19
wheat 12, 13
wheatgerm 13
working drawings 7
work order 8

Y
yoghurt 19

*I'm an orange guppie.
Don't eat me or there'll never be any of me left.
*sniff**

(do you think it's working?)
(think so — one of them's crying)
(OK... *ahem*)

Oh, woe is me — for I am the orange guppie and I'm being overfished...